Anglo-Saxon Kingdoms

A Captivating Guide to the History of Wessex and Mercia

Free Bonus from Captivating History (Available for a Limited time)

Hi History Lovers!

Now you have a chance to join our exclusive history list so you can get your first history ebook for free as well as discounts and a potential to get more history books for free! Simply visit the link below to join.

Captivatinghistory.com/ebook

Also, make sure to follow us on Facebook, Twitter and Youtube by searching for Captivating History.

Contents

Part 1: Wessex

A Captivating Guide to an Anglo-Saxon Kingdom of England and Its Rulers Such as Alfred the Great, Edward the Elder, and Athelstan

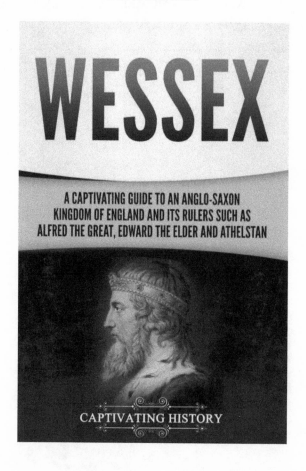

Introduction

The Golden Wyvern of Wessex

*https://upload.wikimedia.org/wikipedia/commons/thumb/4/47/
Wessex_dragon.svg/1280px-Wessex_dragon.svg.png*

The Anglo-Saxon Kingdom of Wessex was created through conquest by the Germanic tribe known as the Gewisse. For the following five hundred years, this kingdom went through various transformations. Some even argue that those transformations were nothing more than the natural development of a society. However, while the other Anglo-Saxon kingdoms prospered and rose to be a significant power in the region just to fall from grace and be consumed in the events of the period, Wessex pressed on. It, too, came close to its downfall when it seemed that Mercia, a neighboring kingdom, would prevail in the constant struggle for domination. However, Wessex showed that it could thrive even under the pressure of other, much stronger forces.

One of the main reasons for the success of the West Saxons was its leadership. A series of strong kings ruled this kingdom, expanding its borders, maintaining prosperous alliances, and leading their people into a better future. Wessex was one of the richest kingdoms, and it is no wonder that law and education prospered here. The kings of Wessex understood the significance of the written word, and it is from here where most of the written records come, and these records survived the ages to tell us their stories.

The *Anglo-Saxon Chronicle*, written at the court of King Alfred the Great, is one of the main sources of information for scholars about the entirety of medieval England. Alfred's law code gives insight into the laws of the previous kings of Wessex but also those of Mercia and Kent. The medieval West Saxon rulers understood the significance of the world around them. They gathered and preserved information about significant people and other kingdoms that interacted with their own. Due to the marvelous work of the West Saxon monks and scribes, we can put the pieces together and create a large picture of what medieval England was like.

Wessex started its expansion during the 8th and 9th centuries, and at first, it encompassed all the lands south of the Thames. The kings of the West Saxons became overlords to all the smaller kingdoms around their heartland. Some were absorbed into Wessex while others continued being independent, although they had to recognize the authority of the kings of the West Saxons. Some were still defiant, but it wasn't long until the Vikings arrived as well. The Danish raids altered any plans the kings of Wessex might have had about continuing their expansion. The pillaging and notorious brutality of the Vikings left a deep scar in the Anglo-Saxon world. Some kingdoms were unable to defend themselves, while others bought their peace. One by one, the Anglo-Saxon kingdoms fell once the Danes changed the nature of their attacks from raids to organized warfare. They were here to stay and work the land, as well as raise their families. England had only two options—to succumb or to defy the newcomers.

The first to fall was East Anglia, followed by Northumbria and Mercia. Wessex remained as the last Anglo-Saxon kingdom, and if it wasn't for the capable leadership of Alfred the Great, it too would have fallen. And what a sequence of events that was. Alfred was the youngest of five brothers, so he shouldn't have had any chance to rule. However, a series of events that occurred made it possible for this young scholar-king to take the throne. With the keen mind he had, Alfred realized he wouldn't be able to defend his kingdom if a change in the Anglo-Saxon world didn't happen. His reorganization of the army and the whole kingdom led to a decisive victory over the Vikings. He didn't just beat the Danes: Alfred the Great set the scene for further conquest. He created the opportunity for his successor to go even further in their intentions and unite the kingdom, which was an opportunity Athelstan recognized and took seriously. England was united, and even though it would face the challenges of renewed Viking attacks, the Anglo-Saxon kingdoms would always strive to unite in the future.

And what of Wessex? It survived. Wessex transformed from a Germanic pagan kingdom to the center of power in the whole of England. It is a kingdom that continues to inspire even today. Wessex still exists as a historical and geographical region, sparking respect through its symbols and representation. A golden dragon is still flying, commemorating the former glory of a past kingdom.

Timeline

410: Western Roman Emperor Honorius officially declares that the cities of Britain need to take care of their own defenses. The end of direct Roman rule in Britain.

Late 4th century: The Anglo-Saxons launch their raids in Britain.

Circa 490: The Battle of Badon; Celtic British win against the Anglo-Saxons.

495: Cerdic comes to Britain.

519: Cerdic founds Wessex and reigns as its first king.

534: Cerdic dies and is succeeded by Cynric.

Circa 560: Cynric dies; Ceawlin becomes the king of Wessex.

592: The Battle of Woden and the building of the Wansdyke. Separation of Anglo-Saxons in the east and the rest of Britain.

592: Ceawlin is deposed; Ceol becomes king of Wessex.

597: Ceol dies; Ceolwulf inherits the throne of Wessex.

611: Cyneglis becomes king of Wessex.

628: The Battle of Cirencester, where Cyneglis was defeated by Penda of Mercia.

630: Cyneglis is baptized; Wessex becomes a Christian kingdom.

642: Cenwealh takes the throne of Wessex and marries Penda's sister, Seaxburh.

672: Cenwealh dies; his widow becomes the first and only woman to rule Wessex.

674: Escwine becomes the king of Wessex.

676: Centwine takes the throne of Wessex.

685: Caedwalla becomes king of Wessex. He attacks Sussex and the Isle of Wight and commits genocide on the island.

686: Caedwalla takes control over Kent.

689: Caedwalla abdicates and leaves for Rome, where he dies. Ine becomes king of Wessex.

694: Ine writes the Wessex law.

705: Wessex gains control over Surrey.

710: Ine fights against Dumnonia.

715: The Battle of Woden's Barrow.

722: Ine attacks Sussex. Wessex loses the Battle of Hehil against the Britons.

726: Ine abdicates the throne and leaves for Rome. Ethelheard becomes king of Wessex.

733: Mercia invades Wessex and takes Somerset. Mercia's overlordship of Wessex begins.

740: Cuthred becomes king of Wessex.

750s: Wessex gains independence.

756: Cuthred dies.

757: Cynewulf becomes king of Wessex. Ethelbald of Mercia dies; Cynewulf retrieves the northern Wessex territories.

779: The Battle of Bensington, where Wessex is defeated by Offa of Mercia.

786: Beorhtric becomes king of Wessex under the overlordship of Offa.

802: Beorhtric dies; Ecgberht is crowned king of Wessex.

815: Wessex attacks Dumnonia.

825: The Battle of Ellandun; Wessex defeats Mercia.

829: Ecgberht invades Mercia and drives its king into exile.

830: Mercia regains independence.

836: The Vikings attack Wessex. The Battle of Carhampton takes place, which Ecgberht loses against the Danes.

838: The Battle of Hingston Down takes place, which Wessex wins against the Vikings. Wessex annexes Dumnonia.

839: Ecgberht dies; Ethelwulf becomes king of Wessex.

849: Alfred the Great is born.

850 or 855: Ethelwulf goes on a pilgrimage to Rome and brings Alfred with him. Wessex co-ruled by Ethelwulf and his son, Ethelbald.

851: The Vikings attack Wessex; Ethelwulf defeats them.

858: Ethelwulf dies; Wessex is divided with Ethelbald ruling Wessex and Ethelberht ruling Kent.

860: Ethelbald dies; Ethelberht takes the throne. Ethelberht unites Wessex and Kent once more.

865: Ethelred I, Ethelbald's and Etherlberht's younger brother, becomes king of Wessex.

866: The Vikings conquer York and Northumbria.

867: Mercia comes under Viking attack.

869: The Vikings attack and conquer East Anglia.

870: The Vikings attempt to invade Wessex but are expelled from the kingdom.

871: Ethelred I dies; Alfred, Ethelred's younger brother, becomes the king of Wessex.

874: The Vikings expel King Burgred from Mercia.

876: Renewed Viking attacks. Alfred is unable to repel them.

878: The Vikings attack Wessex; Alfred escapes. Later in the year, Alfred wins in the Battle of Edington against the Vikings.

878: Alfred the Great and Guthrum make a treaty. Guthrum accepts Christianity and takes the name Ethelstan. The treaty also defines the borders of the Danelaw, and Alfred becomes the king of the Anglo-Saxons.

888: Guthrum dies.

892: The Vikings attack Wessex.

896: Alfred builds a fleet and defeats the Vikings, who give up on conquering Wessex.

899: Alfred dies; Edward the Elder becomes the king of Wessex.

902: Battle of Holme after Ethelwold, Edward's cousin, and the Vikings invade Mercia. The Vikings win.

906: Edward makes peace with the Danes.

909: Wessex and Mercia attack the border of Northumbria.

910: The Battle of Tettenhall takes place; the Northumbrian Vikings submit to Edward.

918: Ethelfled, Lady of the Mercians, dies; the Mercians submit to Edward.

924: Edward dies; Athelstan, Edward's son, becomes the king of the Anglo-Saxons.

926: Athelstan meets with Sitric Cáech, the king of the Vikings in Northumbria. Athelstan receives submission of the Northumbrian Vikings.

927: Athelstan becomes king of the English; Wessex is no more.

929: Athelstan dies; the united English Kingdom falls apart.

Chapter 1 – The Transitional Period

Even though the Roman rule of Britain ended in the early 5ᵗʰ century, their presence remained in the form of education, law, and economy, and it was the elite of the British society that insisted on old Roman traditions. They rebuilt Roman villas and baths, and they, at times, even built completely new ones that were still based on Roman designs. Water ran through the pipes of households during the sub-Roman period. Literacy in the Latin language survived mainly because of the dominant religion of Christianity. However, it was the elite's insistence of continuing the Roman way of life that helped maintain Latin influence beyond the Church.

Even though the Western Roman Empire, to which Britain belonged, withdrew all their troops from the island, the majority of its inhabitants considered themselves to be Romans. As such, Britain continued to be a part of the culture that was the Roman world. It's possible the Anglo-Saxons were already present in Britain during this sub-Roman period as mercenaries who were called to help fight off the "barbarian attacks" of 408. This transitional period of Britain between the Roman rule and the rule of the Anglo-Saxons is usually observed as a period of Britain's decline. But not all of Britain suffered the same fate at the same time. Different parts had different problems to deal with, as well as different methods of survival in order to cope.

For some time, Wessex continued its Romanized everyday life. The evidence suggests that Winchester continued to be one of the major towns or forts of this region. During the 4th century, this town was flourishing as it attracted not only the merchants and craftsmen but also by the elites of the society, who built their rich residencies on the outskirts. However, with the decline of Roman rule in Britain, these residencies, together with the villas in the countryside, were either abandoned or repurposed into storage rooms. Wessex may have experienced a major economic crash during the early 5th century, and it was easier for its people to go back to a simpler way of life.

The towns of Wessex didn't just simply cease to exist, however. They continued to prosper well into the 5th century, but signs of the decline of town life can be seen shortly after. Archeologists discovered a layer of black earth covering the villas on the outskirts of Winchester and similar towns in Wessex. This is a sure sign of the decomposition of Roman timber used to build these villas, as well as the plant life overgrowing on top of it. The same was the fate of Roman pottery and tools. However, people didn't just stop using them. They continued to use them in the British Isles well beyond the early 5th century. However, these items were not produced anymore. It was not because people didn't know how but because they needed to revert to more simplified versions to be able to afford their production. Britain didn't enter a downfall due to the fact the Romans left; rather, it was due to the economic crisis that followed, and many historians speculate that it would have happened even if Rome continued to rule.

The late 4th century had seen the increase of taxes in the British Isles, which were imposed by Roman emperors who fought wars in faraway lands. Small farmers had to overproduce to be able to pay these taxes, and the majority simply couldn't keep up with the demand. In the cities and among the elite, the economic crash wasn't felt at first, probably because it was in these cities where the coin circulation had to continue. Also, it is the elite of the society who collected the taxes, which most likely helped them to accumulate their wealth too. However, the more the Roman demand for taxes grew, the more the British economy suffered, causing the collapse of its society. Even the cities were not able to keep up with the demand, and they, too, started their downfall. Once the Roman influence vanished, so did the trade they brought with them. Many previously wealthy families of merchants and town administrators had to settle for much simpler lives. Plenty of them even abandoned the cities in search of food in the countryside.

In Wessex, specifically, all regions suffered equally, and as such, the disappearance of the Roman way of life affected them all. It is, therefore, not safe to presume that the arrival of the Germanic tribes to the shores of eastern Wessex was the event that sparked the change. In fact, the change had started much earlier with the economic crisis and the abandonment of the Roman way of life.

But Germanic tribes did bring another change with them. They might not have directly influenced the downfall of Romanized Britain, but they did affect its material culture and social values. This new influence is evident when we compare early 5th-century burial sites of eastern Wessex to western Wessex. The shires of the western territories, such as Devin, Dorset, and Somerset, lack the burial sites of the Germanic type, while eastern territories, such as Berkshire, Hampshire, and the Isle of Wight, have them dating from the late 4th century. This is why the eastern and western territories of Wessex have to be regarded separately when it comes to the pre-Saxon period.

The Arrival of the Anglo-Saxons

https://en.wikipedia.org/wiki/Angles#/media/
File:Britain_peoples_circa_600.svg

Gildas the Wise, a monk who lived and worked in 6th century Britain, wrote *De Excidio et Conquestu Britanniae* ("On the Ruin and Conquest of Britain"), a religious tract in which he blames the downfall of Britain after the Romans left on the non-Christian lives of his contemporaries. Even though his work is not regarded as history but as a religious sermon, he does mention the Saxons as an overseas enemy who brought harsh judgment on his people, a judgment they deserved for not following the Christian doctrine. Gildas gives us an explanation of how the Saxons came to be in Britain in the first place as well. After the Romans left, Britain suffered from the attacks of the Scots and Picts, and in order to defend their territories, a council of local rulers, which Gildas calls "the tyrants," decided to give the eastern lands to the Saxons in exchange for their protection. The late 4th-century burial sites of eastern Wessex suggest that it could be this territory that was given to the Saxons initially. The main ruler of the council was a man who Gildas named "superbus tyrannus" (which may be translated as the arrogant or proud tyrant), and he is identified as King Vortigern in later sources.

Gildas also informs us that the Saxon mercenaries who inhabited the eastern territories complained about the lack of food. When the kings of Britain didn't listen and refused to send them food, they broke the treaty and attacked the territories across the whole of Britain. The first war between the Saxons and Britain lasted for nearly thirty years, starting with the Battle of Badon. Gildas tells us he was born in the year of this battle, which makes him the source who might have had firsthand information on the events. The battle was a victory for the Britons (Britons were the Celtic people native to the British Islands), and they successfully stopped the spread of Anglo-Saxons throughout Britain. Legend has it that the mythical King Arthur participated in this battle. Sadly, the lack of sources makes it almost impossible to conclude the exact date, location, and other details regarding this battle.

By Gildas's account, it was Ambrosius Aurelianus who led the Britons to victory in the Battle of Badon. He was a military leader and a Christian whose parents were slaughtered in the initial Saxon attack. He gathered other survivors of Saxon raids and formed an army mighty enough to stop their further conquest of Britain. Ambrosius is the only man from the 5th century who Gildas mentions by name. It is important to mention that it wasn't Gildas who linked King Arthur to the Battle of Badon, though. The Arthurian legend comes from the 9th century, and its author is possibly a Welsh monk named Nennius, who certainly didn't live at the time of this battle; therefore, he is not a reliable source.

What followed the Battle of Badon was an extensive period of peace, in which Gildas lived. It was this peace that brought the unjust rule of tyrants who lived in luxury and self-indulgence. The criticism Gildas made in his work *De Excidio et Conquestu Britanniae* was pointed toward his contemporaries, and it is no wonder he does not name all of them. He does name some, though, and in doing so, he attached an insult to the name. For example, he speaks of a certain Aurelius Caninus (Aurelius the Dog-like), but we cannot connect this name to any of the known kings who ruled Britain during this period. This is because, for Gildas, the historical facts were just a byproduct of his sermon. Instead, he intended to speak up against the rule of kings. And he did not limit himself to one kingdom; he was concerned with the whole of Britain, regardless of language or ethnicity.

Gildas also complained about the partition of the country, as its eastern parts were given to the enemy. Shrines in the Saxon territories were unavailable to the pilgrims of Breton origin (Celtic people native to the historical region of Brittany, today's western France), and this is where Gildas sees the fall of his country. He blames the leaders for abandoning the eastern parts, but he also calls for a civil war or an uprising of the people to bring justice back to the territories that were still under their claim.

The second source widely used by historians to interpret the events regarding the settling of the Anglo-Saxons is Bede's *Historia ecclesiastica gentis Anglorum* (the "Ecclesiastical History of the English People"), which dates to around 731 CE. Bede carries the title of the "Father of English History" because his works, even though filled with biblical commentary, are historical in nature. He used Gildas's writing as his source but also other contemporary writers that did not survive. Bede was a Northumbrian, and so, his work is biased as he wrote with the intent to represent other Anglo-Saxon kingdoms in a worse light. However, his division of the Anglo-Saxon settlement in three phases might have a better historical background than Gildas's suggestion of an invasion.

Bede speaks of the exploration phase, in which the Saxons came to Britain as mercenaries on the invitation of the warlord Vortigern, who employed them to defend the kingdom from Scots and Picts. After the exploration phase came the migration phase. Twenty-first-century scholars have developed a theory that states a great migration of the peoples happened due to climate change. It was this climate change that was responsible for the lack of food in the Anglo-Saxon country of origin, as well as possible floodings, which urged the people to migrate and seek new lands. The third phase, Bede explains, started when the newcomers, the Anglo-Saxons, took control over the territories of Britain. This is the phase in which the Saxons gained political dominance over the Bretons.

The only source of Anglo-Saxon origin that speaks of their migration and settlement on the British Isles is the *Anglo-Saxon Chronicle*, which dates from the 9th century. More precisely, the original manuscript was created during the reign of King Alfred the Great, probably in Wessex. However, none of the manuscripts that survived are originals. The *Anglo-Saxon Chronicle* is a collection of manuscripts, and they are all copies of one original, which were then distributed to various monasteries for preservation and further updates. Some continued to be updated even six hundred years after the original was created. Even though it is a historical document, it is hard to discern which version is to be trusted as the manuscripts differ from each other, even when they are mentioning the same events. But the advantage of the *Anglo-Saxon Chronicle* is that it notes some events that were unknown to Gildas or Bede. These events are used to fill in the gaps and offer alternative views when studying Anglo-Saxon history.

No matter which of the sources is taken into consideration, all of them agree that the eastern territories were given to the Saxons and that it was where they based their invasion of the rest of the country. There is evidence that would support this division of Bretons in the west and Saxons in the east. Around the same year as the Battle of Woden (592), a dike was built that separated the eastern Saxon lands from the rest of Britain. This dike is known as Wansdyke, which comes from the Saxon Woden's Dyke, and it is an earthwork that served as the border between the British Celts and the West Saxons.

Modern archeology suggests that the dike was built at a much earlier time, and its sections date from the Roman period. That would mean that when the Saxons took control of the land, they just renamed the existing dikes in honor of their God Woden, also known as Odin.

The Earliest Anglo-Saxon Territories and Culture

Three Germanic tribes settled in Britain: the Angles, Jutes, and Saxons. The *Anglo-Saxon Chronicle* speaks about a legend that says they came in three ships, each landing in a different place in Britain. The Angles landed on the territories that would later be known as East Anglia, Northumbria, and some parts of Mercia. The Jutes came to the lands known as Kent and the Isle of Wight, while the Saxons took over what would become Wessex and southern Mercia. However, the Britons made no distinction between these Germanic tribes, and Gildas named them all Saxons. Later, Bede used the term "Angli" to describe all three tribes. The Anglo-Saxon name came into use during the 8th century when the need to distinguish continental Saxons from those of England arose. Anglo-Saxon came to mean English Saxons, and as such, it has been in use ever since. The Christian Church preferred the term "Angli" for the people, and it stayed in use even during the reign of King Alfred the Great (r. 871–899) of the West Saxons.

Anglo-Saxons rarely called themselves by this name, though. They made tribal differences, and at the beginning of their settlement of Britain, they used local clan names such as Mierce, Cantie, Gewisse, Westseaxe, and so on. Some of these names would be preserved in the geographical names of kingdoms or towns. In fact, it was the Angli who gave the name to modern-day England, and their language, Englisc, known to us as Old English, went through modernization to become today's English language.

Within Wessex, it was the valley of the River Thames that offers the earliest evidence for Germanic settlement. Some historians speculate it was the clan or the tribe named Gewisse that originally inhabited these parts of Britain and that the term West Saxons came into use at a later date when this tribe took control of other peoples who inhabited the area. The River Thames and its surroundings became what would later be the traditional heart of power for the Anglo-Saxon kingdoms. It is almost impossible to tell the exact borders of each of the tribe's domains, though, as they often fluctuated over time. In the same manner, it is impossible to pinpoint a date when any of the Anglo-Saxon kingdoms started its existence.

The first ruler of the Gewisse tribe that Bede mentions in his *Historia ecclesiastica gentis Anglorum* is Ceawlin, but he also observed that he was the second of the great overlords. This means he had a predecessor who was probably as equally powerful as he was. However, all Anglo-Saxon royal families tended to spread the belief that they had an ancestor who was a famous hero and who was probably somehow related to Woden. The Mercian royal house has a mythical ancestor Icel who was supposedly the one who led the great migration. The East Anglian dynasty claims they are the descendants of Wehha, who was possibly a hero from the old English poem *Beowulf* and who was tied to the old Swedish royal family. The house of Wessex originates from the hero Cerdic, the first king of Wessex. The *Anglo-Saxon Chronicle* claims he was a direct descendant of the god Woden.

The Anglo-Saxon tribes started uniting into kingdoms sometime during the 5th century. It is widely believed that it was the position of the Anglo-Saxon peasants that created the opportunity for the beginning of kingship. The Anglo-Saxon peasant, known as a ceorl, was a free man with certain rights, such as protection under the law and owning land. A ceorl had his kinsmen as support, and he worked the land but also carried arms in times of need. The ceorls were grouped around one overlord to whom they paid rent or provisions in return for leadership during crises. It was these groupings of working individuals that created the basis for the existence of kingdoms.

Larger kingdoms were established by the end of the 6th century, first on the southern and eastern shores of Britain. Although the exact borders are not known, they included the Jutes of Hampshire and Wight, the South Saxons, the East Saxons, and the Angles of Lindsay, Deira, and Bernicia (lands north of the River Humber, which would later become Northumbria). It is possible that these kingdoms created their first bases on territories that were previously occupied by the Romans. It may be that they used the old Roman network of roads and towns. By the end of the 6th century, the Anglo-Saxon overlords started acting as kings. Bede uses the term *bretwalda* to describe a warrior leader who had dominion over a group of people and who was able to establish a system of tribute payments. The *bretwalda* also offered protection to the small regions that were inhabited by people who paid him tribute. All Anglo-Saxon *bretwaldas* claimed their descendancy from Woden one way or another, making it seem as if it was a condition of some sort when imposing their rule over others.

Anglo-Saxons were pagans when they came to Britain, as they had brought their religion with them. By the time of the Anglo-Saxon arrival, Britain was already accepting Christianity. During the late 4th century, Christianity had its centers in the major towns. But in the countryside, the old Celtic polytheistic religion still bloomed. Some areas of Wales lacked any evidence of Christianity until the early 5th century. With the arrival of the Anglo-Saxons, the Britons who mingled with them adopted their religion as a way of progressing in society. Anglo-Saxon paganism is probably the same as the belief system of other northern European countries. Sadly, there is no written contemporary evidence as the first Anglo-Saxon settlers were illiterate. The only source for their pagan religion we can find is in the writings of later Christian monks. However, they never described the pagan belief system of the Anglo-Saxons as they were not interested in it. Their goal was to represent it as evil, and as such, they didn't bother to go in-depth while describing it. Other sources that can help to determine the old pagan religion of the Anglo-

Saxons are mostly of archeological nature. The most evidence we have today comes from the excavation of Anglo-Saxon burial sites.

The conclusion is that the Anglo-Saxon tribes believed in deities known as *ese*, with Woden (Odin) being the most prominent. Other significant gods were Thunor (Thor) and Tiw (Tyr). All the names of the gods are the Germanic version of the old Norse religious system. The Anglo-Saxons also believed in many other supernatural beings, such as elves and dragons, which helped them explain natural phenomena. The Anglo-Saxon belief system probably included the practice of some form of shamanism, which was probably deeply rooted in magic and witchcraft. The Anglo-Saxon kingdoms converted to Christianity during the 7th and 8th centuries, though, with each kingdom doing so at its own pace.

Chapter 2 – The Creation of the Kingdom of Wessex

According to the *Anglo-Saxon Chronicle*, the first king of Wessex was Cerdic, who was one of the first settlers to come to Britain. Cerdic and his son Cynric landed with their five ships on the shores of Britain in 495, where today's Hampshire lies. Upon arriving, they fought the Briton king Natanleod at Natanleaga. Cerdic and his Saxons were victorious, although the fighting lasted for thirteen years. In 508, they killed Natanleod along with his five thousand soldiers. Cerdic founded Cerdicesleag, which is presumed to be today's Charford, where, in 519, the Anglo-Saxons defeated the Britons. Tradition has it that Charford means "Cerdic's ford" and that Natanleaga is today's village of Netley Marsh in Hampshire. However, scholars believe that King Natanleod never existed as his name is a product of etymological reinterpretation. Indeed, Natanleaga was the name of a geographical territory, and its element *naet* means wet, as this area was a marsh. This doesn't mean there was no Briton king to defeat. It simply means that his name was not preserved.

Historians don't rely heavily on the *Anglo-Saxon Chronicle* when it comes to the founding of the Wessex royal dynasty for the simple reason that archeological evidence supports the Jutes to be the first settlers of these regions. The *Chronicle* is not consistent, and some of its manuscripts describe the same events differently. For example, in some versions, the Jutes were given the Isle of Wight by Cerdic's son, Cynric, who was their ally. In another version, the Jutes' first kings, Wihtgar and Stuf, were Cerdic's nephews, while the third version claims the Jutes first landed on the Isle of Wight with King Wihtwara as their leader. Wessex was also supposedly founded by the Germanic tribe Gewisse, but this name simply means "ally." One theory suggests that the Gewisse were, in fact, the allies of the Jutes, but whether it was another Germanic tribe or the Britons remains unclear.

The name of King Cerdic is also problematic as it seems to be of Brittonic origin. Scholars think of it as a Germanic form of the Briton name Ceretic, which is a familiar Celtic name (for instance, Ceretic of Alt Clut was the king of Scotland from the 5th century). One theory is that Cerdic was a native Briton whose family integrated into the Anglo-Saxon society very early, possibly even as early as the 4th century. This theory is supported by the fact that some of Cerdic's descendants also had Briton names, such as Cedda or Caedwalla (Cædwalla). The other possibility is that Cerdic comes from the Anglo-Saxon family who inhabited Britain before the great migration and who accepted this Celtic influence. This would explain his familiarity with the Anglo-Saxon society well enough to become their leader but still be influenced enough by the Britons to keep their name and to even pass it on to his descendants.

When the *Anglo-Saxon Chronicle* first mentions Cerdic and his son Cynric, it names them as ealdormen, and it binds them to the year of 495. It is possible that they were the representatives of an old Briton noble family that possessed the lands that were under Anglo-Saxon attacks. As ealdormen, they were tasked to defend these lands, and this element of the *Chronicle* supports the theory that Cerdic and the dynasty he founded in Wessex was, in fact, of Briton origin.

As an independent ruler, Cerdic is mentioned only in 519, which suggests that this was when he ceased being a Briton vassal and started his own kingdom. It is possible that Breton Cerdic developed blood relations with the invading Saxons and Jutes, who named him and his men "Gewisse", or "allies." Some scholars even go further to prove Cerdic's Briton origin and claim his father was Elesa or Elasius, who was the chief of the region during Roman Britain. There is a minority among historians who believe that Cerdic is a purely fictional character who was created by later Anglo-Saxon kings of Wessex to justify their family ties with Woden and the territories they ruled.

Once Cerdic began his rule, he tried to expand his kingdom. There is evidence that suggests the Saxons attacked a British stronghold, Badbury Rings, across the River Avon. It seems that the attack was unsuccessful, and the expansion of Cerdic's Wessex was halted for the next thirty to fifty years. It is possible that at the same time the Battle of Badon happened, the peace agreement between the Anglo-Saxons and the Britons was achieved. This would certainly stop any further attempt of the expansion, at least for the time being. Even though Gildas claims the Saxons were defeated in this major battle, the *Chronicle* fails to give any report about the defeat.

The *Anglo-Saxon Chronicle* notes that Cerdic died in 534 and that he was succeeded by his son, Cynric, but the Genealogical Regnal List, which is a preface to the *Chronicle*, mentions a certain Creoda. It is possible that Cynric was, in fact, Cerdic's grandson and that his actual son, Creoda, ruled very shortly. Because his name is never mentioned in the body of the *Chronicle*, some scholars claim he never existed and that his name is just an addition to the list of rulers to expand the royal family.

The origins of the Kingdom of Wessex are more complex than what surviving sources of later dates suggest. We cannot truly pinpoint the date of the beginning of Cerdic's rule simply because the *Chronicle* is a very unreliable document with many versions that contradict each other. Some historians even suggest that Cerdic ruled from 538 until 554 based on what the written sources claim. Others suggest that Cerdic was a Saxon leader who was defeated at the Battle of Badon, which could have happened anywhere between 490 and 518. Certainly, Wessex was an independent kingdom with well-defined borders by the time of the rule of King Ceawlin, who was the son of Cynric. Bede even names Ceawlin as a *bretwalda*.

The expansion of the Kingdom of Wessex continued during the rule of Cynric, who conquered Wiltshire and captured Old Sarum near Salisbury in 552. Together with his son, Ceawlin, he defeated the Britons at Beranburh, also known as Beran Byrg (possibly Barbury Castle), in 556. All of this was noted in the *Anglo-Saxon Chronicle*, the same document that claims Cynric arrived in Britain with his father Cerdic in 495. If all of these years are correct, then King Cynric cannot possibly have been the son of Cerdic, making the rule of King Creoda seem more plausible. However, scholars believe that the dates are not to be trusted as they differ greatly from manuscript to manuscript.

The name Cynric is obviously of Anglo-Saxon origin as it can be directly translated to "kin-ruler." But his predecessor Cerdic and his successor Ceawlin both had Celtic names. In order to fit the narrative, some scholars proposed an alternative etymology of Cynric's name. They claim it is a derivative of the Breton name *Cunorix*, which means "Hound-king." This name already has a history of transforming into the Old Welsh *Cinir* and in the Middle Welsh *Kynryr*. However, there is a theory that claims that Ceawlin was not Cynric's son and that the connection was made to tie the ruling Breton family with the Anglo-Saxon name. It is possible they were relatives through the blood-ties of Britons and Anglo-Saxons who intermingled during this period. This blood tie was later transformed into a father-son relationship in order to legitimize the Wessex dynasty.

Ceawlin and the Expansion of the Kingdom of Wessex

Cynric ruled for 26 years, and Ceawlin inherited the throne at around 560, although the exact year is unknown. Ceawlin ruled at the end of the 6th century, and his role in the final conquest of Britain is of key importance. It is in the *Anglo-Saxon Chronicle* that we can find the details of some of the important battles that gave Wessex its first form. Ceawlin was the leader of these campaigns, which occurred along the River Thames Valley going as far as Surrey in the east and to the west at the mouth of the River Severn. The dates of the battles are noted in the *Chronicle*, but it seems they are inaccurate, which is often the case when it comes to this document.

In 554 (according to the *Chronicle*), Ceawlin fought his first battle against the Britons at Beran Byrg (Bera's stronghold) with his father, Cynric. However, Ceawlin was the king during the next battle, which occurred in 568 at Wibbandun (current location unknown). In this battle, he fought King Ethelberht (Æthelberht) of Kent, which made this battle the first conflict between the Saxons. All previous battles recorded by the *Anglo-Saxon Chronicle*, Bede, or even Gildas are battles between Anglo-Saxons and Britons. At Wibbandun, Ceawlin was victorious, and he drove his enemy back to Kent.

In 571, a certain Cuthwulf fought a battle against the Britons at Bedcanford. During the battle, he conquered Limbury, Aylesbury, Benson, and Eynsham, but he also lost his life. It is unknown what relation Cuthwulf was to Ceawlin, but it is presumed they were of the same royal line of West Saxons. The territories that were acquired during this campaign are all mentioned to be Breton, but it is very strange that the Bretons held any lands so far to the east during this period. It has been suggested that Cuthwulf simply reconquered the territories that were lost during the Battle of Badon.

According to the *Anglo-Saxon Chronicle*, in 577, Ceawlin, together with a man named Cuthwine, killed three Breton kings—Coinmail, Condidan, and Farinmail—in Dyrham. With the death of these three kings, the West Saxons took the cities of Gloucester,

Cirencester, and Bath. It is unknown who these three Breton kings were, as their names are in the archaic form and possibly transcribed from an earlier source that is lost to us. This battle must have been the key moment in the West Saxon expansion as the Britons were now divided west of Severn from their people who lived south of the Bristol Channel. This is the same territory Wessex later lost to Penda of Mercia, probably in 628, who then founded the Kingdom of Hwicce.

The last recorded victory of the West Saxons under the leadership of Ceawlin was in 584. This was the Battle of Fethan Leag, after which Ceawlin took many towns. It is speculated that Fethan Leag is, in fact, a forest named Fethelee, which used to be in the territory of today's Oxfordshire.

In his *Historia ecclesiastica*, Bede mentions Ceawlin as the second to hold imperium over the kingdoms south of the River Humber. The term "imperium" is freely translated as "overlordship," and this would mean that Bede considered Ceawlin a *bretwalda*. This is confirmed later in the *Anglo-Saxon Chronicle*, which contains a list of all of Bede's *bretwaldas* with the addition of the later king of Wessex, Ecgberht. Bede also tells us that Ceawlin was a pagan and that he was not Christianized. The first to do so was Ethelberht of Kent, who lived at approximately the same time as Ceawlin. Ethelberht is listed as the next *bretwalda* in Bede's work, but this doesn't mean he ruled after Ceawlin. Their rules probably overlapped at some point, as we have evidence that they warred against each other in 568, at least according to the *Anglo-Saxon Chronicle*. It was after this battle that Ethelberht managed to gain enough power to be considered a *bretwalda*. It might be that Ceawlin's defeat in 592 brought the opportunity for the king of Kent to rise to power.

The year 593 is noted as the year of Ceawlin's death. The *Chronicle* speaks of a great battle at Woden's Barrow (today's Adam's Grave in Wiltshire), where Ceawlin was defeated in 592, with his death following the next year. There is no mention of who his enemies were, nor are any other details of the battle given. Since Ceawlin lost his throne in the year of the battle and not in the year of his death, historians speculate that it was Ceol, the next king of Wessex, who plotted against him. Other scholars prefer to think it was an alliance of the Angles and Britons who had a powerful enough army to challenge *Bretwalda* Ceawlin. There is a possibility that Wessex was fragmented at this point as well because of the surviving grandsons of Cynric, Ceol and Ceolwulf. It is presumed that the brothers were based in Wiltshire while Ceawlin had his base in the upper Thames Valley. It must have been this split of Wessex that influenced the rise of King Ethelberht of Kent.

Even after Ceawlin's death, Wessex continued to be a military power, as there is evidence of successful battles against Essex and Sussex approximately twenty years after his death.

Dynastic Turmoil, Acceptance of Christianity, and the Rise of Mercia

The next king of Wessex was Ceol, who was most likely Ceawlin's nephew, and he reigned from 592 until 597. Ceawlin had a son who should have succeeded him, Cuthwine. However, the fact that Ceol took the throne in the same year as the Battle of Woden's Barrow speaks in favor of the theory that there was a dynastic struggle for power. Cuthwine joined his father in exile after the battle, and it is believed that during the short reign of Ceol, he lived as an outlaw. However, when Ceol's brother, Ceolwulf, took the throne, Cuthwine based his family in the upper Thames Valley, deepening the fragmentation of Wessex. It is believed that the strong families of Devon and Gloucestershire also contributed to the fragmentation as their leaders didn't want to bow to Ceol's rule.

Cuthwine lived a long life, and he must have been a powerful figure during the reign of Cynegils, the son of Ceol, and then Cenwealh, the son of Cynegils. Cuthwine was present at the negotiations with King Penda of Mercia, who, together with his sons, overran the kingdom in 645. However, nothing else is known about Prince Cuthwine except that after the line of Ceol ended in 685, it was his descendants who took the throne.

In 611, Ceolwulf was succeeded by Cynegils, who ruled for 31 years, according to the *Anglo-Saxon Chronicle*. It is possible that by 614, he shared the rule with a certain Cwichelm, but some prefer to think Cwichelm was his son. Bede mentions Cwichelm as the king of Wessex who ordered the assassination of Edwin of Deira in 626. Even though the *Chronicle* gives the impression that Wessex was always ruled by one king, it is quite possible that they often shared the rule with other powerful representatives of the royal family. Whatever their connection was, both Cynegils and Cwichelm fought Penda of Mercia in the Battle of Cirencester in 628, which they lost. Penda took the territories of the Severn Valley and the Kingdom of Hwicce, which had been in the Gewisse's control since Ceawlin took them from the Britons in 577. Cwichelm was last mentioned in the *Chronicle* when he was baptized in 636, as he died the same year.

Cynegils was baptized even earlier in 630 by Bishop Birinus, who established his bishopric at Dorchester. King Oswald of Northumbria acted as a godfather to both Cynegils and Cwichelm. Cynegils's baptism was the first conversion to Christianity ever recorded by a West Saxon king. However, Christianity did not yet spread throughout all the territories of Wessex. In fact, Cynegils's son, Cenwealh, wasn't baptized until much later, after he took the throne in 642. Nevertheless, Wessex was now officially a Christian kingdom, even though the people remained pagan for some time. It is possible that Cynegils agreed to convert in order to form an alliance with the king of Northumbria, Oswald, who married Cynegils's daughter after the king of Wessex was baptized. This alliance was needed to fend off Penda, the king of Mercia, who had already taken some of the territories that belonged to the West Saxons.

Penda's attacks marked the beginning of Mercia's expansion, and the constant pressure they placed on the northern territories of Wessex made its king look to the south for aid. Cenwealh, who succeeded his father in 642, married Penda's sister (or daughter according to other sources), probably intending to repair the relations with the Mercians. Bede tells us that at this time, Cenwealh was still a pagan, and he abandoned his wife so he could take another woman. This angered Penda, who attacked Wessex and drove Cenwealh into exile. It was at the court of King Anna of East Anglia, who had taken him in, that Cenwealh was finally baptized.

Cenwealh came back to Wessex and took the throne once more, probably after Penda's death. Even though he didn't manage to return the territories Wessex had been deprived of by the Mercians, he did expand his kingdom at the expense of the Britons by taking Somerset. Penda's successor, Wulfhere, continued the Mercian pressure on Wessex from the north, but Cenwealh moved to the south, where, in Winchester, he opened another bishopric. This means he took the lands that belonged to the Jutes, who were now confined to the Isle of Wight. These lands would later become the heart of the Kingdom of Wessex. Eventually, Wulfhere advanced south as far as the Isle of Wight, taking the Meon Valley from Cenwealh's kingdom.

Cenwealh died in 672, and some sources mention his widow Seaxburh as ruling for one year after her husband's death. However, it is possible that, like previous kings, Cenwealh shared Wessex, and so did the queen. The *Anglo-Saxon Chronicle* tells us of her succession to the throne, but for this period of medieval history, it was almost unheard of for a woman to rule in her own right. She is also the only woman who appears on the regnal list of the *Anglo-Saxon Chronicle*. On the other hand, the account of Bede tells us that after Cenwealh's death, the kingdom was divided by his sub-kings. It is possible that the situation in Wessex was much more complicated than what the *Chronicle* suggests. Some scholars claim that Bede intentionally refused to mention Seaxburh as she was Cenwealh's second wife. From Bede's Christian viewpoint, she was an illegitimate wife; therefore, her claim to the throne was illegal.

By 674, Wessex had a king again. It was Escwine (Æscwine), the descendant of Ceolwulf of Wessex and the grandson of Cynric. Escwine ruled for only two years, but he managed to defeat King Wulfhere of Mercia at Biedanheafde (unknown location). In fact, there is no evidence of who won the battle, but at around the same time, Wulfhere died, and thus, the Mercian grasp over Wessex was broken. Therefore, historians have concluded that Escwine was victorious. It is unknown what happened to Escwine, but after only two years, the throne of Wessex was succeeded by Centwine, during whose rule the fragmented Kingdom of Wessex became united once again.

Centwine ruled between 676 and 685 or possibly 686, but it is believed he wasn't the only king of Wessex at this point in history. The only event recorded in the *Anglo-Saxon Chronicle* that concerns Centwine is the mention of him driving the Britons to the sea. However, another source, the *Carmina Ecclesiastica* by the Bishop of Sherborne Aldhelm from the 8th century, mentions Centwine and the three battles he won. Aldhelm also records that this king of Wessex was a pagan at first but that later he accepted Christianity, as he became a patron of the churches of his territories. Centwine abdicated in order to become a monk and was succeeded by Caedwalla.

Chapter 3 – Caedwalla and Ine

During the late 7th century, Mercia's power was such that they did not pressure Wessex only from the north. In fact, Wulfhere, the successor to Penda, raided Ashdown in East Sussex in 661, and then he did the same to the Isle of Wight. He placed this kingdom and the district of Meonware under the rule of King Ethelwealh (Æthelwealh) of Sussex. To confirm the alliance between Mercia and Sussex, Ethelwealh was baptized with Wulfhere acting as his godfather. He also married a princess of Hwicce, which was a satellite kingdom to Mercia. Wessex was in danger of being surrounded by Mercia and its allies, and it was probably at this time that Cenwealh subdued the Jutes of Hampshire. However, Wessex gained permanent control of the Jutes' territories during the reign of King Caedwalla, who ruled from 685 until 688.

During the 680s, Wessex was bordered on the west with the British Kingdom of Dumnonia (today's Devon and Cornwall). To the north lay Mercia, which dominated all the kingdoms of southern England. To the southeast, Wessex bordered the South Saxons (Sussex), and to the east, there were the East Saxons (Essex). Although the exact borders are not known, this was the image of England during the late 7th century. Wulfhere was succeeded by his brother, Ethelred (Æthelred), who had no great military ambitions when it came to Wessex; however, the West Saxons were not able to retrieve the territories they had lost in the north. At this time, Wessex was fighting both the Mercians and Britons in Somerset, Gloucestershire, and Wiltshire, but they did keep their influence in the west and south in Dorset and Glastonbury, where the West Saxon kings acted as the patrons of their abbeys.

Caedwalla was the son of Coenberht and the grandson of Cedda, who was the son of Prince Cuthwine. Through this line of ancestors, Caedwalla was a direct descendant of Cerdic, the first king of Wessex. However, Caedwalla is an Anglicized version of the British name Cadwallon, which suggests he was of Briton descent. It is quite possible his genealogy was later added by the scribes of the *Anglo-Saxon Chronicle* to explain his appearance in the royal dynasty of Wessex. Caedwalla is first mentioned in the *Life of St Wilfrid*, a hagiography from the 8th century, as an exiled nobleman. The exile of West Saxon kings wasn't uncommon during the late 7th century, especially because the kingdom was often ruled by more than one king, causing a constant dynastical struggle for power. Even during his days of exile, Caedwalla was able to draw people to himself and form an army, with which he defeated the king of Sussex, Ethelwealh. But Caedwalla didn't manage to keep the territories he gained with this victory, for soon he was expelled from Sussex by its ealdormen.

Caedwalla became the king of Wessex in 685, and he only ruled for two or three years. Bede claims Wessex was still ruled by divided sub-kings by the time Caedwalla took the throne; however, the *Chronicle* claims it was his predecessor, Centwine, who managed to unite the kingdom. It is generally believed that Centwine began his rule as one of the sub-kings but managed to impose his superiority very quickly. However, there is evidence of the existence of these sub-kings during the rule of Caedwalla, as he granted lands to one King Bealdred, who ruled the area of Somerset and West Wiltshire. Another possible sub-king during this period was Cenred, who was the father of the future king of Wessex, Ine. The charters that granted the land to him are dated to 681 and are considered genuine, confirming that Wessex was indeed still divided.

Even though he only ruled for two, possibly three, years, Caedwalla was a very energetic and active king. As soon as he took the throne, he attacked the South Saxons, killing Berthun, one of the ealdormen who drove him out of the territories of Sussex in his first attempt to claim them. Immediately after, Caedwalla conquered the Kingdom of Wight, which was still a pagan territory controlled by Sussex. Caedwalla committed genocide here, as he intended to resettle the island with his own people. In doing so, he killed nearly every native of the island, and even though the heirs of the Kingdom of Wight fled, Caedwalla managed to find them at Stoneham in Hampshire and executed them. Bede mentions a priest persuaded Caedwalla to allow the heir of the pagan Kingdom of Wight to be baptized before his execution. Bede also tells us that Caedwalla was wounded during this conflict but recovered enough to abdicate and travel to Rome, where he was baptized by Pope Sergius I on the Saturday before Easter in 689. Seven days later, he died, probably succumbing to his wounds.

There are surviving charters dated to 688 in which Caedwalla grants individuals the lands in the area of Farnham, making it evident that by this point, he controlled Surrey. Considering that he might have been the founder of the monastery at Hoo, north of Rochester, it is possible he attacked and controlled Kent in 686. Later, he installed his brother Mul as the ruler of Kent, but a revolt occurred, and Mul was burned alive, according to the *Anglo-Saxon Chronicle*. Caedwalla was angered, and he attacked Kent once more, but instead of subduing it, he ravaged the land and left it in chaos. There is a possibility he directly ruled Kent, but there is no written evidence to support this claim. Either way, he extracted the amount of 30,000 pence from the people of Kent as a compensation for the death of his brother Mul. It is believed that this was the price for the life of a prince according to the Anglo-Saxon law of wergild, a term that refers to the defined value of each man's life.

Caedwalla was a Christian king, but he wasn't baptized until his pilgrimage to Rome. On his way, Caedwalla stopped in Francia, where he donated money for the building of a church. There is also a record of him visiting the court of King Cunincpert of the Lombards (northern Italy). Caedwalla was often described as a pagan king, but this is not necessarily the truth. He wasn't baptized because he most likely wanted to choose his own date and place for the sacred ritual. He was respectful of the Church, as there are charters in which he grants lands for various religious buildings. In the *Life of St Wilfrid*, it is described that Caedwalla sought this saint to be his personal spiritual guide. As if to confirm that Caedwalla was a Christian king, Bede said he vowed to give a quarter of the Isle of Wight to the Church, and there are two charters in which he grants the land on the island to the Church.

Ine (r. 689–726)

When writing about Ine, Bede tells us he was of royal blood, which means he came from the Wessex royal family and was probably the descendant of the first kings. The *Anglo-Saxon Chronicle* follows his ancestry by saying that he was the son of Cenred and that Cenred was the son of Ceowald. There is no further information beyond that, but it is safe to assume Ine was, indeed, the distant descendant of Cerdic. But his relationship with the previous king, Caedwalla, is a mystery. It would seem that Ine did not take the throne immediately after Caedwalla abdicated in 688. This might indicate there was some dynastical conflict before Ine was crowned in 689. It is very likely that the sub-kings of Wessex fought for dominance, and Ine was the one who won it. There is also strong evidence that Ine ruled together with his father, Cenred, for some time and that his father remained a sub-king after Ine gained authority above them all.

During the reign of Caedwalla, the territories of Wessex expanded in the south, while the northern territories were lost due to the Mercian attacks. We have a clear picture of what Wessex looked like when Ine took over the throne. The upper Thames Valley was still under the rule of the West Saxons except beyond the northern bank of the river. To the west, the kingdom reached the Bristol Channel; these territories had belonged to Wessex for over a hundred years before Ine. Caedwalla made himself an overlord of all the southern kingdoms, such as the Isle of Wight, Sussex, and Kent. On the eastern border lie the East Saxons, who controlled London.

Caedwalla left Kent in chaos, but Ine made peace with this kingdom. In 694, the king of Kent, Wihtred, paid Ine what the kingdom was owed for the death of Caedwalla's brother, Mul. The territories in the south were under Ine's overlordship for some time. King Nothhelm of the South Saxons was noted in some charters as the kinsman of Ine. It might be that Ine bound himself with the royal line of Sussex through marriage in order to keep the peace in these territories. There is even evidence that the two kings campaigned as allies in 710, which means that Ine had the South Saxons under his control at this point.

At around the same time, Surrey continued to be a problematic territory, as Essex, Wessex, and Mercia all fought for control over it. The diocese in London had ecclesiastical claim over the territories of Surrey, and it appears that this fact created many problems for the three kingdoms. Finally, in 705, Surrey was transferred to the diocese of Winchester, which gave Wessex full control over it. The letters between Bishop Wealdhere of London and Archbishop of Canterbury Brihtwold, written between 704 and 705, prove that the relations between the East Saxons and the West Saxons were tense at this point. The East Saxons sheltered the exiles from Wessex, which angered Ine and caused the conflict. Ine proposed peace under the condition of Essex expelling those exiles. Bede writes that Sussex was under the control of King Ine for some time before an exile ran to

Surrey in 722, which caused Ine to attack Sussex once more. This exile was maybe Ealdbert, a rebellious member of the royal family who was killed during Ine's campaign in Sussex.

The *Anglo-Saxon Chronicle* informs us that Ine and his kinsman Nothhelm fought the Kingdom of Dumnonia, which was ruled by King Geraint. He was the last king of the unified Welsh territories, and he was killed in the battle against Wessex in 710. This campaign brought Devon under Ine's control, making the River Tamar a new border with Dumnonia. However, there is some dispute over the control of Devon, as there is evidence that Ine fought the Britons again at the Battle of Hehil in 722, which Wessex lost. The exact location of this battle is still unknown, and there are speculations that claim it could have been at Devon, while other scholars think it could have been Cornwall.

In 715, the Battle of Woden's Barrow took place, in which Ine participated, but it remains unclear whether the battle was between Wessex and Mercia or if the two kingdoms were allied against a common enemy, an unnamed opponent. The result of the battle is also unknown. It could be that this battle was Ine's attempt to regain the old territories beyond the northern bank of the River Thames, and if that was so, he did not succeed. The territories of the southern bank remained under the control of Wessex, though, as we have evidence of charters being issued in 687 that concerns lands being given to the church at Streatley on the Thames and at Basildon.

Ine was married to Ethelburg (Æthelburg), who is considered to be one of the Anglo-Saxon warrior women. She is remembered in history for burning down the Taunton stronghold in 722 while she was attempting to discover where the traitor and rebel Ealdbert was hiding. This incident may speak of some dynastical unrest, as the exile Ealdbert was a part of the royal family. Furthermore, the *Anglo-Saxon Chronicle* records that Ine slew someone named Cynewulf. Nothing is known about this person, but his name does suggest a connection to the royal house of Wessex. If the connection between the two events is proven to be true, it would confirm the theory that Ine faced an internal resistance that had to be dealt with.

Ine was a Christian king as well, and it is interesting that during his reign, the first nunneries were opened in Wessex. This was done by Ine's kinswoman, Edburga, the daughter of King Centwine. The second woman who was a key person for opening places of worship for women was Ine's sister Cuthburh; she founded the abbey of Wimborne. She was married to King Aldfrith of Northumbria, but they separated, after which she returned to her brother's court.

Ine abdicated the throne in 726, leaving no obvious heir. Bede records that Ine left his kingdom to the younger men and went on a journey with his wife Ethelburg to Rome. There, both of them died. In the early medieval period, a pilgrimage to Rome was thought to give one a better chance for admission to heaven. It is possible that Ine founded the Schola Saxonum, a charity institution for all the Saxon pilgrims who came to Rome, in 727, but some historians believe it was Offa of Mercia who actually did so. This institution must have played an important role, as Bede informs us that everyone wanted to go to Rome, whether they were a man or a woman, noble or freeman, young or old.

Ine was succeeded by Ethelheard (Æthelheard), who ruled from 726 to 740. He might have been his brother-in-law, but his true ancestry remains unknown. It is even possible Ethelheard was the first king of Wessex who was not a direct descendant of Cynric.

Ine's Law

The first legal codes to survive this period are the ones from 602/603 by King Ethelberht of Kent, as well as ones from the 670s or 680s by Kings Hlothhere and Eadric of Kent. Ine was the first Wessex king whose law survived until today, and it dates from 694, possibly even earlier. At around the same time, Wihtred of Kent issued his law code because the two kings agreed on peace after the payment for the death of Prince Mul. Under these conditions, Ine and Wihtred probably cooperated on creating their laws. The evidence to support this claim is in one clause that is completely identical in the codes of both kingdoms. Another piece of evidence for this collaboration is that the king of Kent often used the term "eorlcund," which is a West Saxon word for noble. This is why both Kentish and Wessex laws are considered to have been issued as a means to reestablish authority in both kingdoms and to promote peace.

Ine's law code did not survive in its original form, and only some small parts of its copies are available today. However, his laws are known to us because Alfred the Great later implemented them in his own code of laws, which were issued during the 9th century. Alfred was careful enough to note which laws in his own code belonged to Ine. There might be some of Ine's laws that are missing, though, as Alfred, in his prologue to his code, wrote that he did not note the clauses of the previous rulers he disliked. As such, we cannot be sure if Alfred's version of Ine's laws is complete since he did not specify what laws he omitted. What Alfred did include in his own code is the prologue to Ine's laws, which includes the advisors who helped the 7th-century Wessex king. These names were Bishop Earconwald, Bishop Hedde (Hædde), and Ine's father, King Cenred.

From the laws themselves, it is clear that Ine intended to promote Christianity. He was a Christian king, and he wrote, for example, that the oath of a Christian is worth more than the one of a non-Christian. He also addresses the rites of baptism and observance, which are not secular issues a king should worry about. But he did write laws that deal with civil issues. For example, all ceorls (freemen) were obliged to fence their land. If one failed to do so, and his cattle wandered to the land of another ceorl, he would be held liable for all the damage his cattle caused. From Ine's legal code, we can also learn that tenants held the land in tenure from the lord, and the relationship between the lord and tenant was in the king's complete control. However, Ine's laws do not deal with the problems of the lords, and they do not offer any solutions for the compliance of the ceorls.

Ine's laws confirm the theory that in Wessex, at least during the 7th century, ceorls practiced an open-field farming system when it came to agriculture. This means that the ceorls had the complete right to the land they rented from their landlords and that the land would be inherited by their descendants. This system of agriculture was widely used throughout medieval Europe, but it seems that not all of Wessex followed it. Devon, for example, was exempted from this law.

Other laws of Ine concern military service and the fines both nobles and ceorls had to pay for avoiding it. This fine was 120 shillings for nobles and 30 shillings for freemen. This law confirms that ceorls were obliged to serve in the army, which was an old Anglo-Saxon practice. Scholars agree that it is logical that the land workers would have had to fight their king's wars, as a defeat in battle could mean going from a freeman to a slave under the new ruler.

There is evidence that before Ine's rule, the laws stated that anyone who was accused of murder must have the support of his kin, who would then swear an oath to clear the accused of the suspicion. Ine changed this law and recorded that anyone accused of murder must have a high-ranking person to swear this oath. Ine's laws favored Anglo-Saxon citizens over the British who lived in Wessex. The price of a Celtic life was half the price of an Anglo-Saxon life. Also, the oaths sworn by the Celts counted less than Anglo-Saxon oaths.

Chapter 4 – Problems in the North

The Rivers Thames and Avon are often seen as the borders between Wessex and Mercia. However, these borders often fluctuated as both kingdoms wanted to control all of the valleys that surrounded the rivers. It is no wonder they couldn't settle on the borders. Rivers and their valleys were an exceptional commodity to the kingdom with their fertile lands and merchant towns. The Thames and Avon were especially significant as they provided the Anglo-Saxon kingdoms with access to the sea and trade beyond Britain. The *Anglo-Saxon Chronicle* gives us the record of some of the most significant battles fought over these areas. However, the most reliable sources are the charters and land grants to the churches. Looking at which king issued the charter shows us under whose rule these territories were. Charters are also often precisely dated, which helps scholars establish a precise timeline for various events.

The borderlands between Wessex and Mercia were often in conflict, and the lands were often too devastated by war to fulfill their potential. For example, Malmesbury, which lies on the Wiltshire bank of the River Avon, was controlled by the kings of Wessex, while Bath, right across the river, was controlled by the Mercian satellite kingdom Hwicce. During the 680s, Malmesbury received land grants from both Mercian and Wessex kings. The Mercians did have a custom of providing patronage to the churches in their enemy's lands in the hopes that they would attract the people to their side. It seems that Malmesbury profited from both sides, though, as the abbey lay on the border. But it seems that the danger of constant war was greater than the benefits, as the Abbot of Malmesbury, Aldhelm, wrote to Pope Sergius I to plead to both Ine of Wessex and Ethelred of Mercia to agree that his abbey would not suffer during their wars.

The upper Thames Valley was the heartland of the Gewisse territory; it was actually where their first settlements were erected. However, this is also the territory they first lost to the Mercians during the 7th century, and it is hard to pinpoint where the new border with the north was. Many scholars suggest Ashdown to be the most objective marker for the border during this period in the Middle Ages. Ine possibly recovered control of Berkshire all the way to the Thames River, but this was based on a wrong reading of the charter, which supposedly granted the lands to the Abingdon Abbey. The current reading of the document suggests the charter did not concern this abbey but rather the minister at Bradfield in South Berkshire. The battle Ine fought at Woden's Barrow against or in an alliance with Mercia might have been for the control of the Vale of the White Horse, the area in between the Thames and the North Wessex Downs.

After the death of Ine, the situation on the northern borders didn't settle. King Ethelbald (Æthelbald) of Mercia invaded Wessex in the heartlands of Somerset in 733. It was this invasion that established Mercian overlordship over the West Saxons and their king Ethelheard (r. 726-740). Cuthred of Wessex (r. 740-756) was obliged to follow the Mercian king in an attempt to subdue Wales. The strongest evidence of Ethelbald ruling over Wessex at this point is the charters in which he, in his own right, granted the lands of Wessex to others. During the early 750s, Cuthred tried to gain independence for Wessex, and although he succeeded, he only managed to hold onto it until the end of his reign. Cynewulf, who became the king of Wessex in 757, was a witness to the charters of Ethelbald, who granted the lands of Tockenham to Malmesbury. Cuthred's reign was a time of turmoil for Wessex, as Ethelbald of Mercia persuaded Prince Cynric, Cuthred's son, to try to dispose of his father. Cynric was killed during this attempt, and it wasn't long before Ealdorman Ethelhun (Æthelhun) raised a rebellion against Cuthred. However, this rebellion was over before 752 when Cuthred gained Ethelhun's trust, and together, they brought independence to Wessex.

Ethelbald of Mercia was murdered in 757, and Cynewulf took advantage of Mercia's dynastic struggle to retrieve territories in northern Wessex. He also annexed some lands of Hwicce, a kingdom that was undergoing the process of complete absorption into Mercia. Cynewulf issued charters in which he granted the lands north of the Avon to Bath, which suggests he was trying to establish his authority over the area of Hwicce. But the dynastic trouble in Mercia didn't last long, and it resulted in Offa taking the throne, who proved to be one of the greatest Mercian kings.

Cynewulf was now facing a dangerous enemy, and in 779, they fought the Battle of Bensington, where the king of Wessex was defeated and forced to give back the territories of Hwicce. Eventually, Offa of Mercia ruled all of the Midlands, and he imposed his overlordship over all of the southern states. He is regarded as the most powerful Anglo-Saxon king that ruled before Alfred the Great.

In 786, the Wessex throne was succeeded by Beorhtric (r. 786-802), probably with the help of Offa, whom he accepted as the overlord of Wessex. Together, the Wessex and Mercian kings ruled, but it was Offa who granted the charters in the borderlands to the north, which implies he took direct control of these territories. Beorhtric married Offa's daughter Eadburg, who is said to have had more power and ruled instead of her husband. She ordered the executions of her enemies in her own name, and even if her husband King Beorhtric didn't agree, she would use poison to get rid of the people she considered dangerous to their rule. Asser, the 9th-century biographer of Alfred the Great, records that Queen Eadburg accidentally poisoned her own husband and was exiled to Francia by King Ecgberht, the successor to the throne of Wessex. She took refuge at the court of Charlemagne, the ruler of the Western Roman Empire, and it was there, in Francia, that she became an abbess. However, Eadburg was accused of fornicating with another Saxon man and was expelled from the monastery. Charlemagne left her on the streets, and she ended her life as a beggar.

Even though Beorhtric was the Mercian puppet king, he used his influence to gain some possessions in the northern border territories. An estate at Purton was given to him, which he restored to Malmesbury. However, he also agreed to give the Glastonbury Abbey to a member of the Mercian royal house, Cynehelm. Berkshire also stayed under Mercian rule, and Offa made sure to pass the family monasteries in the borderlands to the members of his royal family. In this way, Cookham became the possession of his widow, Cynethryth.

After the death of Beorhtric in 802, Ecgberht was crowned as the new king of Wessex. Immediately, he became involved in a war that occurred between Hwicce and Wiltshire. After a decisive battle, North Wiltshire and Somerset were finally recognized as a part of the Kingdom of Wessex. Even though there is no record of Glastonbury officially being part of Wessex at this point, there is no more mention of its monastery belonging to the Mercian royal family. The northern border of Wessex was restored to its previous shape in the late 7th century. Bath and its monastery remained in Mercia's possession, while Malmesbury remained a part of Wessex. However, from this point on, at the beginning of the 800s, Wessex started its expansion, while Mercia was facing the beginning of its decline. However, the conflict in the north was far from over.

Chapter 5 – The Expansion of West Saxon Power

Ecgberht (r. 802-839)

It is hard to trace the genealogy of Ecgberht as it varies depending on what version of the *Anglo-Saxon Chronicle* you look at. The oldest version, known as the *Parker Chronicle*, is what historians take as being the closest to the truth. According to this version, Ecgberht was the son of Ealhmund of Kent, and through him, he was the descendant of the unknown Eoppa and Eafa, who were the sons of Ingild, the brother to King Ine of Wessex. The genealogy continues further to Cerdic, the founder of the Wessex dynasty. However, this genealogy is often disputed; it is thought that the claims he was of Kentish origin and that his connection to the Wessex royal family were manufactured to create legitimacy for his rule.

If Ecgberht was of Kentish origins, it is quite possible he was forced to run to Wessex when he was very young, as Offa of Mercia subdued Kent and even possibly annexed it during the late 780s. Ecgberht would have remained a threat to Offa as he was the rightful heir to the Kentish throne. Ecgberht tried to take over the throne of Wessex after the death of Cynewulf in 786; however, he was defeated by Beorhtric, who most likely had Offa's help. Ecgberht was forced to live in exile, and he took refuge at the court of Charlemagne in Francia for the next three years. It is possible that instead of spending only three years in exile, he spent thirteen, and the first number might have been an error in the *Anglo-Saxon Chronicle*. Beorhtric ruled for sixteen years, and it is very unlikely Ecgberht would have been allowed to return to Britain during that time.

Charlemagne may have even helped Ecgberht win the throne of Wessex once Beorhtric died in 802. Some even speculate he had the help of the pope himself, but there is not much evidence to support this, except the fact that the pope always supported Charlemagne. The Mercians continued to oppose Ecgberht, and the Kingdom of Hwicce attacked the Wessex territories of Wiltshire on the very day of Ecgberht's accession. The Wessex ealdorman of Wiltshire was victorious, though, and there is no further record of Ecgberht's relations with Mercia for the next twenty years. There is also no evidence that he ever submitted to Mercian rule, and it is quite likely Ecgberht had no influence beyond the borders of his kingdom. It is generally believed that Ecgberht maintained the independence of Wessex but couldn't impose his overlordship on the southern kingdoms. During the next few years, Ecgberht focused on his campaigns with the Welsh, and in 815, he ravaged the lands of Dumnonia (Cornwall), where he would return on a second campaign ten years later.

One of the most important battles in the history of the Anglo-Saxon kingdoms took place during the reign of Ecgberht of Wessex. The Battle of Ellandun (also spelled as Ellendun) took place in 825, where Beornwulf of Mercia was defeated by the king of Wessex. The importance of this battle lies in the fact that after this defeat, Mercia's supremacy over the southern kingdoms started its decline. The place of the battle is recognized to be today's Wroughton in Swindon. The *Anglo-Saxon Chronicle* gives us a description of the battle, and it records that Ecgberht sent his son Ethelwulf (Æthelwulf) to lead the armies of Wessex against Baldred of Kent. Ethelwulf defeated

Baldred, and the *Chronicle* records that at this point, all the men of Kent, Sussex, and Essex bowed to Ethelwulf. Here, the *Chronicle* gives a comment that the people recognized they had been wrongfully divided from their Wessex relatives. This passage probably refers to King Offa of Mercia, as he had annexed Kent before Ecgberht's rule during the 780s. The *Anglo-Saxon Chronicle* doesn't give detail who was the aggressor in the Battle of Ellandun, but historians agree that it must have been Beornwulf, who took the advantage to attack during Ecgberht's campaign in Wessex that same year. It is possible the threat of unrest in the southern kingdoms motivated Beornwulf to attack and try to secure Mercia's dominance in the southern territories.

After this battle, Mercia lost its power in the south; however, this wasn't the only consequence of the Battle of Ellandun. The following year, East Anglia asked Ecgberht for protection against Mercia, as Beornwulf had attacked them with the intention to recover his overlordship of that Anglo-Saxon kingdom. Beornwulf died in this attempt, and so did his successor, Ludeca, who attempted an attack on East Anglia a year later in 827. Mercia couldn't foresee the outcome in East Anglia, and instead of reaffirming their dominance, they lost it all to Wessex. It was Ecgberht now who was the dominant power in the southeast and who was the real threat to Mercia.

Ecgberht moved fast, and in 829, he invaded Mercia, which was ruled by Wiglaf at the time. He drove the Mercian king into exile and took control of London, where he issued his own coins as the direct ruler of Mercia. Once Ecgberht took control of Mercia, he was referred to as a *bretwalda* in the *Anglo-Saxon Chronicle*. Ecgberht was the eighth *bretwalda* in the history of the Anglo-Saxon kingdoms, and he only appears in the *Chronicle*. This is because Bede died in 735 before Ecgberht's rule, and thus only lists seven. In the same year, the king of Northumbria, Eanred, submitted to the rule of Wessex. It is likely that Northumbria didn't submit of their free will, as the later chronicler Roger of Wendover from the 12th century notes that Ecgberht raided the country before they submitted. However, the *Chronicle* doesn't mention these events, and it is unknown which source Roger of Wendover used in his writings.

Only a year after the invasion, in 830, Mercia regained its independence, as Wiglaf managed to take the throne once more. There are no recorded events that would explain how Wiglaf managed to regain his kingdom, but it was most likely due to the rebellion of the Mercian nobles against the rule of Wessex. It is also possible that, at the same time, East Anglia regained its independence, as its king, Ethelstan (also spelled as Athelstan or Æthelstan), minted his own coins during this period. It seems that after Wessex had its sudden rise to power during the 820s, it could not keep the acquired territories under its control. Historians have tried to understand the reason behind this failure, and one of the proposed theories is that it was the support of the Carolingians that helped Wessex climb to overlordship and that the lack of their assistance must have caused the downfall of Wessex. The most probable reason for the lack of support during the 830s is the rebellion that happened in Francia against their king, Louis the Pious, due to the collapse of the trade network of the kingdom. Once the Carolingians stopped meddling in the politics of Britain, Mercia, Wessex, and East Anglia had to find a balance of power on their own.

However, Wessex did manage to change the geopolitical scene of Anglo-Saxon England as it managed to gain control of the southeastern kingdoms. Essex probably remained under Mercia's control, but East Anglia managed to finally gain its independence. Ecgberht annexed Sussex and Kent into Wessex, and they never gained independence again. At first, they operated as sub-kingdoms of Wessex, but soon enough, they were fully integrated. However, Mercia remained a constant threat to Wessex, and to counter its influence over the northern border territories, Ethelwulf, the son of

Ecgberht, issued charters in which he granted the lands and estates to Canterbury Christ Church.

It was during the reign of Ecgberht of Wessex that the Vikings attacked, and the kingdom was defeated by the Danes in 836 in the Battle of Carhampton. The Danes allied themselves with the Western Welsh people, but Ecgberht managed to win a victory in 838 at the Battle of Hingston Down in Cornwall and regain the territories that had been previously lost. Dumnonia was one of the last British kingdoms that were still independent at this time, but after this battle, it ceased to exist. At this point, the settlement of the Anglo-Saxons in Cornwall began, and even though no written record speaks of this process, some conclusions can be drawn by the names of certain places. The new border was the River Ottery, and all the places south of it remained named in Cornish style, while to the north, most of the places were heavily influenced by the Anglo-Saxon settlers.

Ethelwulf (r. 839–858)

Ecgberht died in 839 and was succeeded by his son, Ethelwulf. However, Ethelwulf had already ruled as a sub-king, as he was appointed to Kent in 825 after the Battle of Ellandun. When Ethelwulf took the throne in 839, his oldest son, Ethelstan, was already old enough to be appointed as king of Kent, and he ruled it until his death in 852. With the crown, Ethelwulf inherited his father's great wealth, which he had acquired during his conquests of Mercia, the southern kingdoms, and Wales. Ecgberht used part of this wealth to secure the Church's support for the accession of his descendants. He bribed the archbishop of Canterbury, and in return, he received a promise that the Church would always support his dynastic line in future struggles for the throne. This implies that Ethelwulf might have had enemies who challenged his succession. However, there is no record of such struggles when it came to be his time to rule.

Ethelwulf's reign was modeled by the Carolingian system of family rule, in which each son would be a sub-king to his father, who was superior over them all. In this tradition, Ethelwulf gave the kingdoms of Kent, Sussex, Essex, and Surrey to his sons when they came of age. However, sub-kings did not have the power to issue charters of their own; they were only allowed to witness Ethelwulf's. He allowed his sons to become witnesses as young as six years old. To secure the support of the local nobles, he appointed them as ealdormen of their respective kingdoms. He chose only Kentish nobles to act as the earls of Kent, the nobles of Sussex areas were the earls of Sussex, and so on. Ethelwulf also gained the ealdormen's support by paying them enough respect, sometimes even ranking them higher in the witness lists than his own sons who were sub-kings.

Ethelwulf showed a friendly face to Mercia, and instead of trying to invade its territories, he offered an alliance against their common enemy, the Vikings. The friendship between the two Anglo-Saxon kingdoms was firm enough for Wessex to help King Beorhtwulf of Mercia to issue his own coins. Ethelwulf allowed the Mercians to produce their coins using the same die-cutters that were used for the minted Wessex coins. Although Wessex coins were issued in Rochester, the same craftsmen issued them for Mercia in London. Further proof of the alliance through these coins comes from the fact that Mercian coinage had the same design on the reverse side as the Wessex coins had on their obverse. However, some speculate that instead of being a sign of the alliance, the similarity between the coins might have been the sign of a forgery or an unskilled craftsman who simply reused Ethelwulf's design.

The alliance of the two kingdoms survived the death of Beorhtwulf and continued during the reign of his successor, Burgred. Ethelwulf helped Burgred regain Mercian control over the Welsh territories, and in 853, he married his daughter, Ethelswith (Æthelswith), to Burgred. Sometime before this, some of the Mercian territories passed under the rule of Wessex, but the circumstances are unrecorded. By 844, Berkshire was still a Mercian territory, but it eventually became a part of Wessex, as Alfred the Great, the son of Ethelwulf, was born on the royal estate of Wantage in Berkshire in 849. This estate wouldn't be considered royal if the territory did not pass to Wessex. However, Ethelwulf continued his practice of appointing local ealdormen in the newly acquired Mercian territories, probably to gain their support and manage the peace.

Ethelwulf decided to go on a pilgrimage to Rome in the 850s at the height of his power. It's speculated that before his departure, he gifted a tenth of his wealth to his subjects. However, there are various charters issued in different years that mention this "decimation" of the kingdom, and since none of them are original, some scholars believe they are frauds. However, the biographer of King Alfred, Asser, mentions the decimation too, and he dates it happening in the year 855. It might be that Asser simply translated what the *Anglo-Saxon Chronicle* recorded about this event and either intentionally chose to translate only some parts or loosely translated it. By all sources, it seems that Ethelwulf left a tenth of his lands to the Church and the people. By people, historians believe he meant tenants, meaning the land was now their personal property. However, it remains uncertain if Ethelwulf did this with his own personal possessions or the land that generally belonged to the kingdom.

By the time Ethelwulf went on his pilgrimage, his sons Ethelbald and Ethelberht were both adults, and so, the king left Wessex in their care. When Ethelwulf departed in 855 for Rome, he brought his youngest son, Alfred, with him. Scholars speculate that since Alfred was the youngest, he was chosen to accompany his father as he was intended for a role in the Church. Another theory is that Ethelwulf chose to bring his youngest son to be affirmed by the pope as throne-worthy. Alfred claimed that Pope Leo IV confirmed him as a possible heir to his father, though historians believe this claim might be propaganda to legitimize his rule over his brother's son.

Ethelwulf stayed in Rome for one year, where he gifted the Roman diocese with a gold crown, two golden goblets, a sword decorated with gold, four silver bowls, two silk tunics, and two veils woven with gold. He also gifted gold to the clergy and silver coins to the people of Rome. Ethelwulf's gifts were rich enough to rival the gifts of the continental kingdoms, as he was showing off the generosity and spirituality of Wessex. Historians agree that Ethelwulf's pilgrimage is very strange. No other medieval king felt safe enough to leave his kingdom for such a long period and hoped to return without facing any problems. Even more odd is the fact that Wessex wasn't safe at all at this time due to the constant Viking threat. The only explanation scholars found for Ethelwulf's pilgrimage is that maybe he was driven by his religious views. Maybe he considered this pilgrimage was needed to placate God's wrath, who had sent the Vikings to punish England for its sins.

On his way back to Wessex, Ethelwulf stayed with the Frankish king, Charles the Bald, and there he married his daughter Judith, who was only twelve or thirteen at the time. All of his sons were by his previous wife, and he had no children with Judith. This marriage was strange, even to the contemporaries of King Ethelwulf, for three reasons. First, Frankish princesses were almost never married to foreigners; they were more often sent to nunneries instead. Secondly, Judith was anointed as a queen. This practice was reserved for the empresses of the Western Roman Empire, and Judith was the first queen to be anointed. The third reason lies in the Wessex custom of not allowing queens to rule. The king's former wife in Wessex never had the title of a queen, and she never ruled as an equal to her husband. She was simply the king's wife and nothing more.

Upon his arrival in Wessex, Ethelwulf had to face the revolt of his second son Ethelbald, who did not want to allow his father to recover the throne. The reason for this, according to historians, is Ethelwulf's marriage to the Frankish princess. It is possible that her anointment meant that at least part of Wessex would be inherited by her sons, and this must have sparked Ethelbald's resentment toward his father. The rebellion ended with Ethelwulf agreeing to part with Kent and allowing his son Ethelberht to rule as its rightful king, while Ethelbald became the co-ruler of Wessex. It may be that Ethelwulf agreed to this because he was afraid that a civil war could ignite and divide the kingdom even more.

Ethelwulf died on January 13th, 858. The division of his kingdom continued after his death, as was intended. Ethelbald ruled Wessex, while his brother, Ethelberht, ruled Kent and the territories to the southeast. Queen Judith brought great prestige to the kingdom as a Frankish princess, and in order not to lose it, Ethelbald married her, to the horror of the Church as she was his step-mother.

After Ethelbald died, which happened only two years after his father's death, Judith sold her possessions and returned to her father's court in Francia. There, she met Baldwin I, Count of Flanders, but Charles the Bald wouldn't allow her to marry him. The couple escaped to the north with the help of Judith's brother, Louis, the heir to the Frankish throne. Charles was so angry that he had his bishops excommunicate the couple and forbade any kingdom to shelter them. In response to her father's acts, Judith and Baldwin traveled to Rome, where they persuaded Pope Nicholas I to cancel their excommunication and acknowledge their marriage. Finally, Charles the Bald accepted his daughter's marriage, and the couple had a son, who later married Elfthryth (Ælfthryth), who was Ethelwulf's granddaughter and the youngest daughter of Alfred the Great.

Chapter 6 – The Royal Brothers

Ethelwulf had a will prepared when he died, which left his kingdom divided between his two eldest sons. His will did not survive the ages; however, Alfred's did, and it mentions his father's intent. The kingdom was to pass to whichever of his sons survived, Ethelbald, Ethelred, or Alfred. Ethelberht was exempt as he ruled Kent, and it was presumed his heirs would inherit that kingdom. However, scholars cannot agree if this will was intended for the whole kingdom or the king's personal possessions. Some even claim both, while others argue that it was unlikely for the whole kingdom to be passed down by a will. Some historians argue that if Ethelwulf left the kingdom in his will, it would have definitely lead to fratricide in the dynastic struggle, which did not happen. It is more likely that the brothers made a deal between themselves to pass the throne to each other. But Ethelwulf's movable riches, such as money and horses, were divided between his children and the nobles. In addition, one-tenth of his hereditary land was to be given to the poor for the salvation of the king's soul. In addition, Ethelwulf ordered three hundred gold coins to be sent to Rome each year.

Ethelbald (r. 855–860)

Ethelbald was the second son of Ethelwulf and his first heir, as Ethelwulf's oldest son, Ethelstan, had died in the early 850s.

Ethelbald ruled alongside his father for the last two years of his life, although some historians see this arrangement differently. The *Anglo-Saxon Chronicle* doesn't record what happened in the kingdom after Ethelwulf's return from Rome. The only source of the events we have is Asser's biography of Alfred the Great, and in it, he claims that Ethelwulf divided his kingdom to avoid a civil war. The most common opinion is that Ethelwulf allowed Ethelbald to rule Wessex together with him, while Kent and the eastern provinces of Essex, Sussex, and Surrey were under the rule of his brother Ethelberht. Other scholars don't agree and prefer to think that the division of the kingdom went even further. They believe that Ethelbald kept his power base and court at Selwood while Ethelwulf ruled only the east of the kingdom, and Ethelberht kept Kent. There is even a third opinion that suggests Ethelbald kept the sole rule of Wessex while Ethelwulf took back Kent and the eastern provinces from Ethelberht.

When Ethelwulf died in 858, Ethelbald continued his rule of Wessex as the sole ruler. As mentioned above, Ethelbald married his step-mother, Queen Judith, but the *Anglo-Saxon Chronicle* ignores this marriage and does not record it. Asser condemned this relationship as well, calling it disgraceful to God. By his words, not even the pagans practiced such marriages. It is possible that the *Chronicle* avoids mentioning the marriage because its prestige would cast a shadow over the greatness of Alfred, during whose reign this document was written. However, other than Asser's condemnation, it seems that the marriage wasn't opposed during the reign of Ethelbald. The Frankish *Annals of St Bertin* does mention the marriage but without any comment on its validity. However, it does tell us how, upon her return to the court of Charles the Bald, she was treated with all the honor of a queen.

The first record of Ethelbald survives in the charter of 840, where his name is written in the list of witnesses as *filius regis* (the king's son). He also appears in other charters with the titles *dux filius regis* and sometimes only as *dux* (ealdorman). The *Anglo-Saxon Chronicle* first records Ethelbald when he accompanied his father in the Battle of Aclea, where, together, they defeated the great Viking army. However, little is known of the period where Ethelbald ruled alone as only two charters have survived. The first one is from 858, and it is a grant of an estate at Farnham to the king by Swithun, the bishop of Winchester, to the king. According to some historians, this means that Ethelbald confiscated the lands of the bishop for his own personal use. The second charter is dated from 860, and it is a grant of land by the king to his thegn (a rank of the aristocracy that fell below ealdorman) named Osmund. Queen Judith was a witness for both of these charters, which had never been practiced before in Wessex since the king's wife had no real power.

Ethelbald died in 860, but the reason for his death is unknown. There is not much left as evidence of his reign, but his reputation suffered due to his rebellion against his father and his marriage to his step-mother. These accusations are first recorded in Asser's writing, and later historians and chroniclers took this stance against him as well. Ethelbald is generally remembered as a weak king who achieved nothing, with Wessex suffering from a period of lawlessness during his reign. It is not known whether he had any children, but if he did, they are not mentioned in any of the sources.

Ethelberht (r. 860–865)

Ethelberht was the third son of King Ethelwulf, and he inherited the throne of Wessex upon his brother's death. He had already ruled Kent and the eastern provinces, and thus, the throne of Wessex allowed him to unite the kingdom once again under one king. His first appearance in the medieval records is in the charter of 854, only a year before his father divided the kingdom before his pilgrimage to Rome. After Ethelwulf's return, Ethelberht continued to reign in Kent, probably as a sub-king. In 858, he became the sole king of Kent, Surrey, Essex, and Sussex by his father's wish.

Once Ethelbald died in 860, Ethelberht succeeded the throne to the Kingdoms of Wessex and Kent. It is possible that Ethelred and Alfred were supposed to inherit the throne of Wessex since Ethelberht had been exempted from his father's will since he already ruled Kent. However, it seems that both of his younger brothers were too young to take the throne, and the crown passed to Ethelberht instead. At this time, Wessex was under the threat of Viking attacks, and it would have been of questionable wisdom to appoint children as its rulers.

Ethelberht refused to appoint a member of his family to rule Kent and the eastern provinces; instead, he chose to unite the kingdoms. It was in the first year of his rule that he issued a charter with witnesses from both Wessex and Kent. This is the first charter of the united kingdom, and as such, it represents a significant point in English history. It contains the names of the archbishops of both Canterbury and Rochester and the names of the bishops of Sherborne, Winchester, Selsey, and London. Ten ealdormen were named from both Wessex and Kent, making this charter unique as it represents the unification of the west and east kingdoms under one rule.

The *Anglo-Saxon Chronicle* tells us that Ethelberht reigned in "harmony and great peace," and it seems that at this point, the brothers agreed that the rule of Wessex should pass among them and not to their sons. The second important charter dates from December 863, in which Ethelberht granted Sherborne Abbey immunity from royal and judicial services. This charter was written in Old English, not in Latin, as was the custom. It could mean that by this time, the transition from Latin to vernacular had already happened, at least when it came to legal documents. Alfred notes that by the time he began his reign, Latin was barely in use anymore.

In the autumn of 865, Ethelberht died and was buried at Sherborne Abbey in Dorset. The cause of death is unknown. Like with his predecessor, there is no record of Ethelberht having any children. Thus, the throne passed to the fourth son of Ethelwulf, Ethelred.

Ethelred I (r. 865–871)

The most notable event of Ethelred's rule must have been when at the Witan (an assembly of nobles and leaders), Alfred asked him to give him his share of the property their father had left to all of his sons when he died. Ethelred answered that he could not divide the property and give Alfred what belonged to him; instead, Ethelred promised he would leave everything to his younger brother after he died. Scholars are still speculating if they were talking about their family's private properties or the whole kingdom. It is possible that Alfred, as the younger brother, wanted to rule Kent and the eastern provinces, as his brothers had during the rule of their father. If this was the case, it is possible Ethelred did not wish to divide the kingdom and make it even more vulnerable to Viking attacks. So, instead, he promised to pass the throne to his younger brother and not to his son. In addition to this argument between the brothers, Alfred rarely shows up as a witness to Ethelred's charters, which might imply they were not in the best relations.

Another important event that occurred during Ethelred's rule is the arrival of the Great Heathen Army in East Anglia. It was at this point that the Viking attacks changed in nature. Instead of just raiding and taking the riches back to their Scandinavian lands, the Danes decided to settle in England. The full invasion of the Anglo-Saxon kingdoms started in the very first year of Ethelred's rule. Although Wessex was not yet directly threatened by this great Viking army, it was just a matter of time. Ethelred tried to help his brother-in-law, Burgred, the king of Mercia, but even together, they were unable to repel the Vikings from Nottingham.

The first attempted invasion of Wessex was in 870 when the Danes took over Reading, a town between the Thames and Kennet Rivers. Ethelred and Alfred were unable to defeat the Vikings there and were forced to flee. But the Danes didn't have their victory over

Wessex yet, as both Ethelred and Alfred were still alive and planning a counterattack. Only four days later, their armies met again in battle, and this time, the West Saxons successfully expelled the Vikings out of their kingdom.

Ethelred died in 871 sometime after Easter. The cause of death is not known, but it can be speculated he died of a wound since he fought the Vikings often during the final years of his reign. Asser doesn't reveal much about his death as he only records that Ethelred was a king of a good reputation and that he ruled for five years. Ethelred had two sons who would have probably been able to seize the throne if their father had lived until they reached adulthood. But they were too young to rule, and so, Alfred succeeded his older brother. Alfred would eventually become one of the most famous Anglo-Saxon kings, the only one who was titled "the Great."

Chapter 7 – Alfred the Great (r. 871–886)

The youngest son of Ethelwulf of Wessex inherited the throne after his three older brothers, Ethelbald, Ethelberht, and Ethelred. During Alfred's life, the Vikings started raiding the coast of England and changed the nature of their attacks from raids to a full-blown invasion. One by one, the Anglo-Saxon kingdoms fell under the rule of the Danes, who intended to settle their population in the newly conquered regions. It was Alfred's Wessex that stood alone, surrounded by the Viking-occupied lands. In fact, it was the last English kingdom to oppose them. Alfred managed to not just preserve Wessex but also to impose his dominance over England. He dared to dream of an England united under a single ruler and for all of the Anglo-Saxon people to bow to him.

Almost everything we know about Alfred's rule comes from his biographer Asser, a scholar and a bishop who is most known for his work titled *The Life of King Alfred*. In it, Alfred is described as a merciful king of a gracious nature. It is no wonder he was given the epithet "the Great"; however, this was only done in the 16th century during the Reformation in England. Alfred remains the only Anglo-

Saxon king to bear this title, and he was also the first king of England with this title, with Cnut the Great being the only other one.

Childhood

Asser notes that Alfred was born in 849 at the royal estate called Wantage, located in Berkshire. Today, this location is in Oxford. Asser is the main source of the facts known about Alfred's life; however, he might be wrong about his year of birth. The *Anglo-Saxon Chronicle*, which was also written in Alfred's court by his order, notes that he took the throne when he was 23 years old in 871. This would mean his year of birth would be either 847 or 848. But if that is the case, how is it possible that Asser missed a year, especially when he had the knowledge of his contemporaries available, among them the king himself? It is possible that Asser thought Alfred took the throne during his twenty-third year, meaning he was actually 22. This would explain that one-year difference, or maybe Asser was right, and the *Chronicle* miscalculated the year of his birth.

Aside from his birthdate, there is very little we know about Alfred's childhood. His mother, Osburh, was described by Asser as a very religious and noblewoman. He also informs us Osburh was a daughter of King Ethelwulf's butler, who was named Oslac. However, nothing more is known of this woman except that she witnessed one charter in 868, unlike Ethelwulf's second wife, Judith. Alfred the Great later justified the position of Wessex royal women by bringing up the misconduct of a queen at the beginning of the 9th century. He was probably referring to Eadburg, the daughter of Offa, who married the king of Wessex, Beorhtric, and accidentally poisoned him in 802.

It was very unlikely that Alfred would have ever become a king simply because he had four older brothers. Even his name suggests a different intention for their youngest son. While all four of his brothers are named with the beginning "Ethel" ("Æthel" in Old English), which translates to "noble," Alfred's name begins with

"Ælf." This element of the name is unusual for Wessex, but it can be commonly found in East Anglia and Northumbria. It means "elf" or "wise"; therefore, his name can be translated as "elf counsel" or "wise counsel." His name might suggest the intention was for Alfred to finish his schooling and devote his life either to God or to the position of advisor to his brothers. However, this theory about his name might be far-fetched as some scholars believe his parents simply liked the name and that no meaning should be attached to it.

Besides the common skills that were taught to all noble boys, such as riding, fighting, and hunting, Alfred extensively learned writing and English poetry. He was literate in both Old English and Latin and was able to speak and write both languages. Later, during his reign, he founded a school for noble boys at his court. He argued that boys should not stop learning even once they began their military training. Alfred was fond of reading and writing, and his pride was in the constant pursuit of wisdom. He was eager to acquire new skills even later in life, saying that learning is a lifetime activity. It is possible that special attention was given to Alfred's education because he was the youngest child that had no real chance of inheriting the throne and instead would have to spend his life in the service of either God or his brothers. Asser tells us the king had a poor education when he was a child, but this might be untrue and simply propaganda meant to justify the reforms of education Alfred implemented during his reign.

The most significant event of Alfred's childhood is certainly his two visits to Rome. In 853, King Ethelwulf sent his youngest son to Rome. Asser writes that Pope Leo IV consecrated Alfred as a king and that he even stood as a sponsor to his confirmation. This means that Alfred was sent to Rome when he was only four or five years old. In medieval times, this was too tender an age for such long travels, making it quite intriguing that Ethelwulf chose to take Alfred on such a perilous journey. However, Asser's record of Alfred being consecrated in Rome is either a misinterpretation of the events or propaganda that would give legitimacy to Alfred's rule when Ethelred's sons were still alive. What really happened is obvious from the letter Pope Leo IV sent to Ethelwulf, a letter that was preserved by the 12th-century scribes. In this letter, the pope tells Ethelwulf that his son has been decorated as a spiritual son, as was the custom of Rome.

Alfred was received by Pope Leo, who honored the little boy in order to preserve good relations between Rome and the Anglo-Saxon Kingdom of Wessex. Alfred became the Roman consul with the pope as his sponsor and spiritual father. This was hardly a kingly consecration. This office of Roman consulship had ceased to exist by the mid-9th century, and it continued to live only as a prestigious title for noble families, whose support the pope expected. Some scholars believe that since Alfred was of such a young age, he could have been under the impression of a grand ceremony, like the one where he was being anointed as king. Later, when he recalled this event, his memory might have been influenced by this childhood impression. However, it certainly helped him to believe and represent himself as a ruler directly consecrated by the pope, with the full right to rule the kingdom instead of his nephew Ethelwold (Æthelwold), the son of the previous king Ethelred, as Ethelwold did have supporters who wanted him to rule instead of Alfred.

The second time Alfred went to Rome was as an escort to his father two years later. Ethelwulf went on a pilgrimage while he was at the height of his power, which was an unusual thing to do in the medieval period, especially with the Vikings being such a close threat to his kingdom. Nevertheless, Ethelwulf chose to spend a whole year in Rome and took Alfred with him. It is possible that Ethelwulf took young Alfred to help prepare the boy for a life devoted to God. What better place for a child to discover the love for the Church than Rome itself? A boy would find the splendors of a richly decorated city attractive and maybe willingly devote his life to God's path. And, as the youngest son, Alfred was expected to find a different path for himself.

The King

Alfred inherited the throne after his brother Ethelred died in 871. Even though he left two sons behind him, they were too young to become rulers. The agreement between Ethelred and Alfred was that whichever brother would survive would inherit the properties of the other. It is unclear whether the kingship was a part of these properties. Nevertheless, Alfred became the king and faced a Danish invasion as early as his brother's funeral. While he was dealing with the matters of Ethelred's burial ceremony and installing his own royal office, the Danes attacked, probably taking advantage of the king's death. The Saxon army suffered a defeat as their new king was absent. Asser writes of Alfred as a great warrior who won all his battles. But this is far from the truth as another defeat soon followed at Wilton. This time, Alfred was present, but the Danes pressed the young king into agreeing to pay them. The Vikings then left Wessex with the treasures Alfred paid them, and they wintered in London.

Finally, Alfred could rule properly, as the money he gave the Danes bought him five years of peace. He was the most improbable of all the kings. Besides being the youngest of five brothers, of which four were his predecessors, he was also the frailest of them all, as Asser reports he was sick from a young age. In *The Life of King Alfred*, Asser left detailed descriptions of this illness, and according to the symptoms, some modern doctors have come to the conclusion that Alfred suffered either from hemorrhoids or Crohn's disease. The illness was very unpleasant and painful, with no known treatment in the medieval period. It must have been a wonder for the Anglo-Saxon nobles and the people in general that Alfred was able to rule at all.

During the five years of peace, it seems that Alfred turned his attention from the Vikings in the north to the economy of Wessex. He restored the silver content of the Wessex coinage, which was probably done in order to increase the value of taxes he imposed on his subjects. He might have started a military reform at this point, but it certainly wasn't finished, which the renewed Viking attacks in 876 prove. There are only two charters from this period of peace that survived, but it's enough to give us a glimpse at what was Alfred's concern at the time. In 873, he made a gift of land to a thegn named Erdwulf. The same land was sold in 785 to Erdwulf's friend Wighelm, and it was done in the presence of Alfred. The lands in concern were in Kent, and Alfred probably did this to ensure the support of the Kentish thegns.

In 876, a new Viking attack followed, and Alfred was again unable to repel it. Instead, he tried to convince the Danes to leave. He realized it wasn't enough to pay them and expect them to never return. He needed some equivalent of a Christian oath to keep the Vikings away. However, he knew that the Christian oath meant nothing to the pagans, so he had to find an alternative. Both Guthrum, the king of the Danes, and Alfred agreed they should exchange hostages. Even though he was Christian, Alfred agreed to swear an oath on Thor's arm ring, a sacred pagan relic, in the hopes that the Vikings would not break such an oath this time. Asser was ashamed to admit this pagan ritual that his beloved Christian king undertook, and he chose not to mention Thor's arm ring in his biography. Instead, he only notes that Alfred took an oath on the relics Alfred trusted after God. Luckily, the *Anglo-Saxon Chronicle* recorded the events and mentioned the pagan arm ring.

However, Alfred was disappointed once more. The Danes used the excuse of the oath and the hostage exchange to slip away and escape to Exeter, where they spent the winter. Instead of releasing the hostages, they chose to kill them all. It is unknown why the Danes didn't keep their promises. Perhaps they considered it to be unworthy to keep an oath with the Christian. Or perhaps they simply tricked Alfred and didn't hold the oath as sacred at all. The truth is, there is little evidence of pagan rituals and beliefs among the Danes who came to England, and the little we know is from the writings of sagas from the 13ᵗʰ century. In any event, the effort Alfred invested in finding common ground with the Danes was a failure.

Alfred's Reforms

Alfred wasn't successful in repelling the Vikings from Wessex until 878. It was evident that he could not continue with the old military system of the Anglo-Saxons if he was to win. The strategies of the Viking armies were completely different, and the Anglo-Saxons were no match for the Danes, who had been brought up in a warrior culture that placed emphasis on raiding. While the Anglo-Saxons attacked by advancing the shield wall toward their enemies head-on, the Danes usually sent smaller groups of attackers from their base, which they could always retreat to if the need arose. The Danes also sought weak points in the Anglo-Saxon shield walls and attacked at those points, which would break it. Also, the Danes were very good at enduring a siege, and it seemed they always had the advantage of provisions, as they prepared their bases well in advance.

The Anglo-Saxons were used to open battle where the king would call on the national militia to defend the kingdom or invade an enemy's lands. But the Danes used a strategy involving hit-and-run tactics. They would send smaller parties to raid and plunder, and the king was unable to predict when and where the next attack would be. Therefore, the king was not able to call all the forces at his disposal and to gather all the needed supplies to fend off the Viking raids. As the locals were unable to deal with the raids by themselves, they often deserted King Alfred and conspired with Guthrum. Alfred learned the lessons from his defeats, and immediately after the victory at Edington in 878, he took the opportunity of peace to reorganize his army.

The central piece of Alfred's military reform was the burhs, which were fortifications and fortified settlements that spread throughout the kingdom like a net of strategically important places. Alfred organized 33 burhs spread apart about 30 kilometers (19 miles). This way, the army was able to confront an attack wherever it came from. Alfred invested in building the walls around the towns, digging defensive dikes, and even reinforcing the wooden palisades. Some old Roman towns, such as Winchester, already had walls, but they were in dire need of repair. Each burh was to be supplied by the landowners of the area. The Burghal Hidage, a contemporary document which describes in detail this system of burhs, survived, meaning we have an insight into how Alfred's military lived and worked. Since the Vikings were famous for their naval force, Alfred built twin-burhs, or twin towns, on each bank of a river. These were connected with a fortified bridge, which also had the role of blocking the river pathway for the Viking ships. The Vikings were not used to besieging, and so, they lacked the equipment to do so. This is why Alfred's system of burhs had an advantage when it came to defense.

Alfred also improved the navy of Wessex with the new designs of ships, which he ordered in 896. He began the construction of around a dozen longships with sixty oars. This design was double the size of the Viking ships, and the *Anglo-Saxon Chronicle* describes them as swift, steady, and being able to ride through shallow waters. Although there are no remains of Alfred's ships, scholars think Alfred used the Roman design with high sides, which were designed for battle and not navigation. This design was meant for open sea battles, and the ships proved to be too large for the rivers where the Danes attacked the most.

In the area of law, Alfred the Great issued the so-called Doom Book, also known as the Legal Code of Ælfred the Great. He wrote his own laws in this book but also gathered the laws of previous kings that he found suitable. Alfred also included the law code of his predecessor, Ine of Wessex. In the introduction to his legal code, Alfred wrote how he had a council that advised him on how to reform some of the previously existing laws that he found unsatisfying. Among other kings whose laws he used, Alfred mentions by name Offa of Mercia and King Ethelberht of Kent, who was the first Anglo-Saxon king to be converted to Christianity.

The code of law is divided into 120 chapters, a symbolic number, as it is the age at which Moses died. Moses was a big symbol for Alfred's code because he is looked at as the link between divine and human laws. One-fifth of the book is the introduction, which Alfred wrote by himself, and it can be observed as his reflection on Christian laws. He even includes all ten commandments and some chapters from the Book of Exodus. The crimes described in Alfred's code can almost all be compensated with payment to their lord. In fact, the only one that cannot be paid is the betrayal of a lord. Alfred thought of lordship as a sacred bond between God and man. To betray a lord is equal to betraying God in his eyes, and no amount of money can justify that.

Alfred insisted that the officials of his kingdom who had the role of judges had to be literate; if they were literate, then they would easily be able to seek out the wisdom needed for their jobs. The disobeying of this act would be punished with the loss of their office. Alfred was a great advocate of education in general, and he is to be thanked for the many religious books that were translated to Old English in order to make them more available to the people.

The Viking raids had had a devastating effect on education in England. One of the reasons for this is that the usual place for learning were the monasteries. And it was the monasteries that were first attacked by the Danes. Many noble houses were reluctant to send their sons to monasteries to learn when there was a danger of losing them due to the raids. The second reason is the constant threat of war that hung above their civilization; due to this danger, there was simply no effort made to promote education, as warriors were in greater need than scholars.

Alfred was aware of all these problems, and he lamented the fate of the education system of England. He wrote about people not being able to read and write contemporary Old English, let alone

Latin. He also complained that the quality of the Latin language was dramatically reduced even when used by learned monks who should know better. And from the surviving Latin script, it is observable, even today, the change in the quality of the Latin language, especially in the areas ruled by the Danes, such as East Anglia and Mercia. Wessex still used Old Latin, and it is the kingdom where this ancient language lingered the longest.

Alfred wanted to bring education to the people, and so, he ordered the translation of many "books of wisdom." It is unknown when exactly Alfred ordered this program of translation, but the many books he thought were necessary for all of mankind to understand were translated into Old English. Some he even translated himself, taking great pride in the venture. Among these books were Bede's *Historia ecclesiastica gentis Anglorum* (the "Ecclesiastical History of the English People") and Orosius's *Historiarum Adversum Paganos Libri VII* ("Seven Books of History Against the Pagans").

Alfred also opened a court school in which his own children were to be educated. However, he still allowed the admittance of children of nobles and others of lesser birth. Such a thing had only been done by Charlemagne, who Alfred greatly respected. In court school, the children learned English and Latin, both writing and reading. Alfred recruited scholars from both England and the continent to teach in his court school. The most famous among the Frankish scholars were Grimbald and John the Saxon, while from England, Alfred employed Werwulf from Mercia and Asser from Wales.

The Death and Legacy of Alfred the Great

It is unknown how Alfred the Great died, but the *Anglo-Saxon Chronicle* records it was on October 26th, 899, and by the time of his death, he was fifty years old. It is possible that he died of the illness that had tortured him from a young age. As mentioned before, it was highly likely that Alfred suffered from Crohn's disease, an illness that affects the immune system. This disease occurs in people with a genetic predisposition to it, and it is known that Alfred's grandson, King Eadred, suffered from a similar disease.

Alfred was buried in the Old Minster in Winchester, and from there, his remains were moved to the New Minster and then, in turn, moved to Hyde in 1110. He was buried next to his wife and children. During the 16th century, the Hyde Abbey was destroyed, but the graves remained intact, at least according to the record. It was in the 19th century, during the building of a prison on the same site, that the graves were destroyed and lost. Archeological excavations in 1999 found one pelvis bone, which radiocarbon dating placed as belonging to the correct period of time of Alfred the Great. However, scholars cannot be sure if the bone belonged to Alfred, his son Edward the Elder, or someone completely unknown whose remains happened to be in the same spot.

Alfred was venerated as a saint by the English Christian tradition. King Henry VI tried to have him canonized by Pope Eugene IV in 1441, but he was unsuccessful. Some Catholic traditions do recognize Saint Alfred, but the modern Roman Catholic Church does not. In the churches of England, Alfred is considered a saint and a great hero, whose image is often depicted in stained glass. October 26th is celebrated as a commemorative day in his honor, and it's a feast day.

Alfred is still seen as a pious Christian king, the first to promote the English language instead of Latin, and who started the system of translations in order to make education approachable for the common people. Because of his great desire to spread education all over his kingdom, many educational establishments still carry his name. One such example is Alfred University in New York, which even has its local telephone exchange as 871 in commemoration of Alfred's ascension to the throne. His birthplace of Wantage, Oxfordshire, opened King Alfred's Academy. Because it was believed for many years that Alfred's reform of the English navy was, in fact, the first navy in the territory of Britain, some ships have been named after this king, such as the HMS *King Alfred* under the Royal Navy and the USS *Alfred* under the US Navy.

Chapter 8 – The Great Heathen Army

Viking raids on the territories of Britain started as early as the late 8th century. They were mostly hit-and-run types of attacks focused on monasteries. Their goal was to gather riches and slaves and take them back to their respective countries. However, something drastically changed during the mid-9th century, as the nature of the Viking attacks changed from raids to invasions. It is possible that the sandy Danish land was not fertile enough to grow food for the rising population, causing families to search for new territories that they could inhabit and where they could support themselves through agriculture. These attacks were not happening just in Britain. Some Vikings decided to attack the shores of Normandy. However, the great Danish army landed on the shores of East Anglia. This army was named the Great Heathen Army by the scribes of the *Anglo-Saxon Chronicle*, men who had firsthand experience in facing the invasion.

The army, although sometimes referred to as the great Danish army, didn't consist only of Danes. In fact, it was a coalition of Scandinavian armies, which included Norwegians and Swedes. Due to the mountainous terrain of their countries, which was unsuitable for agriculture, the Norwegian and Swedish Vikings joined their relatives, the Danes, in the invasion of Britain. It was this unified coalition that landed on the shores of England in 865, during the reign of Ethelred of Wessex, Edmund of East Anglia, Ella (Ælla) of Northumbria, and Burgred of Mercia. Kent and Sussex were already a part of Wessex by this time; therefore, they were under the rule of the West Saxon king.

It is unknown what the size of the Viking army was like, as the *Anglo-Saxon Chronicle* uses the term *here*, which is often translated as warband, instead of *fyrd*, meaning army. King Ine of Wessex specified in his law code in 694 that a *here* numbered more than 35 men. It is possible that this term was used more widely during the 9th century and that it was used to differentiate the Viking army from the royal military of the English Crown. Some scholars propose the size of the army was around one thousand men, while others think the number was far greater and that the army consisted of several thousand men. However, if this is true, then we have yet to discover the evidence of the structures that provisioned such a great foreign army in the territory of Britain.

Whatever the truth is about the size of the army, scholars agree on one thing. The Vikings had a custom of joining the warbands of multiple leaders when they had a common cause. These bands would split apart once their task was achieved and the riches were gathered. It is possible that the same happened here and that the Great Heathen Army had more than one leader. The joint armies must have not only consisted of the Vikings from Scandinavia but also the Vikings from Ireland and those who had raided Francia over the past few decades. It is in Francia where the Vikings had discovered how easily the rivers were navigable, which made the inland monasteries and estates vulnerable to attacks. This same tactic was used in the invasion of England. However, the Frankish lords responded by barricading the rivers, making them difficult to raid and causing the Vikings to turn their attention to England.

Legend has it that the leaders of the Great Heathen Army were none other than the sons of Ragnar Lodbrok (also spelled as Lothbrok)—Halfdan Ragnarsson, Ivar the Boneless, and Ubba. The sagas of the north claim that the invasion was launched by the three brothers in order to avenge the death of their father, who had been killed by Ella of Northumbria. However, there is no historical evidence that this ever occurred as history has no evidence that the Norse hero Ragnar ever existed.

The Fall of East Anglia, Northumbria, and Mercia

The Vikings attacked Wessex in 851, and King Ethelwulf defeated them. It must have been a great blow to the Vikings, as they did not want to risk the might and wrath of Wessex again. Instead, they decided to invade England through East Anglia. There, the Danes received horses and payments in exchange for peace. Supplied by the East Anglians, the Vikings turned their attention to Northumbria and York, where they landed their first attack in the autumn of 866. Northumbria was in the middle of a dynastic struggle when the Vikings arrived. The people had disposed of their old king, Osberht, and passed the title to Ella, who was described in later sources as the king's brother. However, there are no contemporary sources to claim this relationship between the two kings. The Viking attack caught Northumbria by surprise, and both claimants to the throne were killed. It was the Vikings who appointed the next king of Northumbria, the puppet ruler Ecgberht. It is not known if he ruled the whole kingdom or just a part of it with the Danes claiming the rest.

Once Northumbria was secured, the Vikings turned back to East Anglia, with which they already had a peace agreement. The first renewed attack against the Anglo-Saxon kingdom happened in the winter of 869 when the Viking army rode through Mercia to reach East Anglia and took Thetford, where they wintered. Almost nothing is known of the rule of King Edmund of East Anglia since the Vikings destroyed all the contemporary evidence. It is just known that he fought the Danes in a battle and lost. He was probably killed during this battle, but the legend of his martyrdom remains. By tradition, the leaders of the Viking army were Ivar and Ubba, and they tortured King Edmund in an attempt to make him renounce Christianity. But Edmund resisted the beating and was finally shot full of arrows. His head was severed from his body and thrown in the woods. According to a legend, the East Anglians found the head by following an ethereal wolf who spoke the Latin words "Hic, hic, hic" (here, here, here) while leading the men to the king's head.

The fall of East Anglia is the first event that the *Anglo-Saxon Chronicle* mentions related to the Viking invasion. Even though Edmund offered horses and paid the Vikings when they first landed on the shores of East Anglia, he was proclaimed a saint almost immediately after his death because he was killed by pagans. At the end of the 9th century, there were even coins issued that had the inscription "sce eadmund rex" (O, Saint, and King Edmund).

The next to be targeted by the Viking army was Mercia, and it came under attack in the autumn of 867. The Viking army conquered Nottingham and decided to spend the winter there. King Burgred of Mercia was married to Ethelswith, the daughter of Ethelwulf of Wessex and the sister to Ethelred and Alfred. Facing the Vikings, he called his brothers-in-law to help him expel them from Nottingham. Ethelred and Alfred came with their armies and laid siege to Nottingham but were unable to draw the Danes out of the city into open conflict. The well-stocked Vikings were able to sit in the city and wait for the siege to break. The Anglo-Saxon army was filled with farmers who, when spring came, had to abandon the siege and go work their farms in order to produce food for the kingdom. Burgred decided to pay the Vikings to leave, and so, Ethelred and Alfred didn't have the chance to battle.

The Vikings came back to Mercia in 874 and drove Burgred out of his kingdom. In his position, they placed Ceolwulf to be their puppet king. Burgred went to Rome after being driven out of his kingdom, where he died. It appears that Ceolwulf did rule without Viking overlordship, at least to some extent, as he issued charters in his own name. And even though the *Anglo-Saxon Chronicle* describes him as the "foolish king's thegn," he was accepted as the ruler by Mercian clergy and nobility, who often witnessed his charters. When the Vikings came back to Mercia in 877, they divided this kingdom between themselves and Ceolwulf, and he ruled independently in the part of Mercia he had been given until 879. Ceolwulf's Mercia was reduced to the northern and western parts of the previous kingdom. It is possible that the *Chronicle* records Ceolwulf as a thegn in order to strengthen Alfred's claim of overlordship over Mercia. After all, the *Chronicle* was written by his orders at his own court, and it may have been a very biased document.

Wessex and the Vikings

Wessex remained the last Anglo-Saxon kingdom that still resisted the Viking invasion. It was constantly under attacks during the 870s, and at one point, it seemed as if it would be impossible to drive the Vikings out. However, Alfred had brought reform to the military, and the Danes were successfully defeated.

But Alfred wasn't always successful against the Danes. In fact, he lost more battles than he won. As soon as Alfred took the throne, Wessex was attacked by a Viking army, which received reinforcements from the Great Summer Army sent from Scandinavia. This army was led by Bagsecg, a Viking leader whose name was first recorded in the *Anglo-Saxon Chronicle*. The joint army settled at Reading in Berkshire, and from there, they attacked the West Saxon army at an unknown place, where the Saxons lost. In May, at Wilton, Wiltshire, Alfred's army was defeated once more. Alfred was forced to pay the Danes to leave. From Reading, the Viking army continued to Mercia to winter in London, and eventually, they took over that kingdom.

With only one Anglo-Saxon kingdom left, the Vikings returned to Wessex by 876. In the meantime, Ivar the Boneless left the shores of England, and he was never again mentioned in contemporary sources. It is believed he retreated to Ireland to rule the Vikings of Dublin. His departure meant the Great Heathen Army needed a new leader, and Guthrum, who would become known among Christians as Ethelstan, the king of the Danes, was the one to step up to the task. It is not known how Guthrum became the leader of the Danish army, but he was ready to attack Wessex by 876, which was when he led the Danish army from Cambridge into Wessex. Guthrum seized the convent of Wareham in Dorset, where Alfred besieged him. However, Alfred wasn't able to do much, and he once again decided to negotiate for peace. This time, he asked for hostages to be exchanged as a guarantee of their peaceful intentions, and even though Guthrum agreed at first, he broke his promise and slew all the hostages on his way to Exeter, where the Vikings spent the winter. Guthrum expected reinforcements to arrive and join his army at Exeter, but fortune was on Alfred's side. The West Saxon king pursued the Danes and laid another siege at Exeter. This time, Alfred had no reason to negotiate a peace, especially since the Viking reinforcements had wrecked their fleet in a storm. Guthrum finally agreed to release some hostages and leave Wessex, and this time, he kept to his word.

However, Alfred didn't manage to permanently get rid of Guthrum. A year later, in January of 878, the Vikings attacked the royal estate at Chippenham, on the River Avon, where Alfred was spending Christmas. Alfred was unprepared, and the Danes had conquest in mind this time, not loot. Therefore, they pillaged the countryside of Wiltshire, Somerset, and Hampshire, and the king of Wessex was unable to defend his lands. Many landowners chose to submit to the Danes once they realized the royal army was not coming to help them. Among those who surrendered were several ealdormen of Alfred. One of these men was even recorded in a charter that gave his lands away since he had betrayed his king and country.

The *Anglo-Saxon Chronicle* tells us that Guthrum subjected Wessex and its people, except for king Alfred. It is unknown how much of the country Guthrum managed to acquire during this invasion in 878, but Alfred was forced to run, and he found shelter in the small marshland village of Athelney. He had the choice of being expelled from his kingdom and seeking shelter in Rome, like his brother-in-law Burgred of Mercia did, or to die at a pagan's hand, thus becoming a martyr like Edmund of East Anglia. However, Alfred chose to stay and fight, and he organized a counterattack from his hiding place in the marshes of Somerset.

The roles were now reversed, as Guthrum now sat in Chippenham like an Anglo-Saxon king, while Alfred became a raider like a Viking, waging a guerilla war against the invaders. First, Alfred reestablished communication with all of the ealdormen of Wessex that didn't surrender to Guthrum. Together, they organized a militia, which, at first, raided the Vikings in order to feed themselves, scout the situation, and remind the people that their king had not abandoned them and was willing to fight for his country. Alfred was also raiding local ealdormen who had joined Guthrum in order to show them that he still had the power to punish them. This clever game of hearts and minds Alfred played gave him the advantage, as Guthrum couldn't hope to rule the kingdom if he had no support from the local nobles, and Alfred made sure he never got that support.

The *Anglo-Saxon Chronicle* reports that Alfred met with all the leaders of his lands with all of their men at Egbert's Stone, located east of Selwood Forest. From his refuge in the marshlands, Alfred managed to raise the armies of the three shires and gather them all in the same spot, from which they launched their carefully planned attack in May 878. From Egbert's Stone, the Wessex army marched to Edington, where Guthrum had barricaded himself. The Battle of

Edington went in Alfred's favor as his army proved to be victorious, but the Vikings retreated to the fortress and prepared for a siege. The Vikings were ready to apply their usual tactics of sitting it out and waiting for the negotiations to begin. However, Alfred already had experienced the Danes breaking their oaths after a treaty was achieved, and he wouldn't allow another Reading to happen. Instead, he sent his army out to pillage and destroy all the food sources the Danes could use to survive the long siege of Edington. Two weeks later, the hungry Danes sued for peace. The Vikings released the hostages and swore their usual oaths, saying that they would immediately leave the kingdom. In addition, they promised Guthrum would be baptized. That was enough for Alfred, and even though it seems that the terms were not much different than in any other treaty, Alfred had acquired the victory on the battlefield that secured the Viking's behavior.

However, it wasn't just Alfred's military organization that provided him with this victory. In the same year, the Viking leader Ubba attacked Wessex in Devon, where he was defeated by the locals at the Battle of Cynwit. Ivar the Boneless and his brother Halfdan Ragnarsson had left the shores of England, and with them, Guthrum lost their support. It was obvious that there was unrest in the leadership ranks of the Vikings, which certainly influenced their willingness to conquer the lands. In addition, Alfred did a great job of inspiring his people, and he gained the support of three shires with his efforts. Such an army, consisting of the people of the three shires, must have been much greater than the leftovers of the Great Heathen Army that Guthrum commanded.

Guthrum was baptized three weeks after the Battle of Edington, and Alfred served as his sponsor. The ceremony took place at Aller in Somerset, and Guthrum's Christian name was Ethelstan. It seems that with this conversion to Christianity, Alfred tried to impose the moral code of the Christians onto the Viking leader in hopes that, this time, Guthrum would honor his oaths. He also settled in East Anglia with the whole Viking army, at least for a while.

In 885, Asser mentions the army of East Anglia breaking their oaths and attacking Kent. But Guthrum is not mentioned by name in Asser's report. What followed the unsuccessful attack on Kent was the Treaty of Alfred and Guthrum, which firmly set the boundaries between Wessex and the Danelaw. But it appears that these boundaries were not geographical but political, as they describe where the rule of Wessex (not the land) stops and Danelaw begins. Even the term Danelaw is of much later origin, as historians needed a single name for the lands that were ruled by Viking laws in comparison to the lands that were ruled by Anglo-Saxon laws. After the treaty, the Danish lands roughly consisted of fifteen shires: Leicester, York, Nottingham, Derby, Lincoln, Cambridge, Suffolk, Norfolk, Northampton, Huntingdon, Bedford, Hertford, Middlesex, and Buckingham.

Alfred reorganized his army and started building his network of burhs, which made it extremely difficult for other Viking armies to profit from organizing raids into Wessex. By 896, the Vikings had ceased to attack; it seems as if they gave up. Some returned to East Anglia under the rule of the now baptized king Ethelstan, while others went to Northumbria. Another group returned to Scandinavia to their respective homes. Alfred's burhs proved to be so successful that they would help serve his successors in retaking the Anglo-Saxon kingdoms ruled by the Danes and uniting them under a single banner.

Chapter 9 – Edward the Elder (r. 899–924)

Defeat of the Danelaw in the 900s

*https://upload.wikimedia.org/wikipedia/commons/4/
4f/Eroberung_des_Danelags.jpg*

Alfred's son, Edward, inherited the crown after Alfred's death in 899. However, even though he was the son of a king, the transition didn't go smoothly because his cousins, Ethelhelm (Æthelhelm) and Ethelwold (Æthelwold), had as much right to the throne as he did. They were the sons of Ethelred, the older brother of Alfred who ruled Wessex before him. Alfred inherited the throne when his brother died because his children were too young to rule, especially considering the kingdom faced constant Viking attacks.

Ethelhelm probably died sometime during the late 880s or early 890s because he suddenly stopped showing up in any records. He had previously witnessed Alfred's charters, and he even appeared in his will from the 880s, but his name does not pop up in the *Anglo-Saxon Chronicle* after this. His brother, Ethelwold, appeared as a witness in only one of Alfred's charters, and in it, it appears he was placed above Alfred's son Edward, meaning he was of a higher status. But Alfred was able to prepare the kingdom for his son's accession, as he promoted men who would support his son to high-ranking positions. He also continued to gift church officials, whose support was crucial for his son. Without the approval of religious leaders, it would be hard for any king to rule. In one of Alfred's charters, Edward signed as *rex Saxonum* ("king of the Saxons"). It is possible his father allowed him to rule Kent as a sub-king in order to prepare him for the succession to the throne of Wessex.

Edward was the second child of Alfred and his wife, Ealhswith. His older sister, Ethelfled (Æthelflæd), had married the ealdorman of Mercia, Ethelred. She would prove to be a good ally to her brother as she ruled Mercia after her husband's death. However, it seems Edward was closer in age to his younger sister, Ethelgifu (Æthelgifu), who became the abbess of Shaftesbury. It is unknown what happened to his younger brother, Ethelweard (Æthelweard). It is recorded that he was given the education to become a scholar, which may indicate that he was meant to join a monastery and become devoted to God. However, his children were recorded, which is proof he didn't join the church. Alfred had one more child, Elfthryth, the youngest daughter, who married Baldwin II, Count of Flanders. Asser records that the princess had the same education as her brother Edward and that she was an obedient and nice child. This marks the first time that Anglo-Saxon history records a princess having the same education as a prince.

While he was still a prince, Edward had the chance to prove himself in military leadership. He led his own troops during the renewed Viking attacks in 893 and 896, and he was successful in repelling them. At around the same time as his first command against the Vikings, Edward married Ecgwynn, his first wife, who gave birth to a son named Athelstan and a daughter whose name remains unknown, but it is known she married Sitric Cáech, the Viking king of Northumbria. Edward married a second time after his father's death to a daughter of Ealdorman Ethelhelm of Wiltshire named Elfflaed (Ælfflæd). It is unknown what happened to Ecgwynn; she might have died by the time of Edward's second marriage, or perhaps she needed to be disposed of due to various political reasons. Some historians even argue that she was Edward's lover and not his wife, but it is strange that her children would then be chosen as successors. Edward married for the third time around 919, this time to Eadgifu, the daughter of the ealdorman of Kent, Sigehelm, who had lost his life in the Battle of the Holme in 902.

When Alfred died on October 26th, 899, Ethelwold seized the royal estates of Wimborne, where his father, King Ethelred, was buried. He also took Christchurch in Dorset in his efforts to oppose Edward's succession. He declared he would rather die in Wimborne then surrender to Edward, who marched against him with an army. However, during the night, Ethelwold sneaked out of the estate and ran to Northumbria, where the Vikings accepted him as the rightful king of York. Supported by the Danes, Ethelwold attacked Mercia in 901, which was the most important ally of Wessex. On December 13th, 902, the armies, led by Edward and Ethelwold, clashed. This event is known as the Battle of the Holme, and both Ethelwold and the Danish king of East Anglia, Eohric, lost their lives during the battle. Despite losing their leaders, the Vikings won the battle, and the Anglo-Saxons suffered heavy losses. But the death of Ethelwold ended the threat to Edward's throne, and the Vikings were not interested in taking the territories.

Alfred received the formal submission of all Anglo-Saxon people that weren't ruled by Danes in 886, and his title after this recognition was *Anglorum Saxonum rex* ("King of the Anglo-Saxons"). As Edward had succeeded his father's throne, he, too, ruled all of the English people, and he used the same title in all the charters he issued except for two. In geographical terms, Edward ruled the whole Kingdom of Wessex, including Kent and the eastern provinces, but also a large part of Mercia. His sister Ethelfled, as mentioned above, was married to a Mercian ealdorman; however, it seems that Edward granted them the right to rule the land on their own. This is why some scholars prefer to think of Ethelfled as the last queen of Mercia. Edward issued charters concerning the land in Mercia, but all of them state that the rulers of this territory were Ethelred and Ethelfled. Therefore, Edward was their overlord, but he did give the couple administrative rule to some extent, as both of them issued charters in their own name.

Edward is probably one of the most neglected Anglo-Saxon kings. The main reason might lie in the fact that few contemporary sources of his rule survived. Scholars used to believe he didn't achieve much and that he didn't deserve any space in the history books. However, in the late 20th century, this opinion changed, and Edward started being regarded very highly. He might have been lesser when it came to administration or education, but his military successes were what set the scene for the United Kingdom of England. His sister Ethelfled played a huge role in conquering the southern Danelaw, and her success overshadowed Edward's in the eyes of scholars. Although Ethelfled deserves all the praise that was given to her through history, Edward was equally deserving. Edward ruled for 25 years, and he didn't just expand the realm of the English people—he also secured relative peace for the next century. The Danes were not so eager to attack once they lost their territories to Edward.

Conquest of the Danes

After the Battle of the Holme, there are no recorded conflicts between the Anglo-Saxons and the Danes. However, there is a record of Edward suing for peace in 906, and although it is not known what happened, this suggests that a conflict existed. The *Anglo-Saxon Chronicle* mentions that Edward made peace out of necessity, which implies he was in a situation where he needed to pay the East Anglian and Northumbrian Danes to leave his kingdom, just as his father Alfred did. For an unknown reason, Edward encouraged the Anglo-Saxons to buy properties and land in the territories ruled by the Danes. This might have been due to an agreement he had with the Vikings or in preparation for returning the lands to Saxon rule.

A combined West Saxon and Mercian army harassed the border between Mercia and Northumbria in 909 until they managed to acquire the bones of Saint Oswald from Bardney Abbey in Lincolnshire. This was probably the idea of Ethelfled, as she started the cult of Saint Oswald in the new minster she founded in Gloucester. Oswald was Ethelfled's predecessor and the king of Northumbria (r. 634–642). She started the cult of Saint Oswald in Mercia to satisfy the needs of the people who had relocated from Northumbria to escape the Viking rule. The Danes were forced to accept the peace with Edward, but they retaliated the very next year. They raided Mercian territories in 910 and were successful until they met the combined West Saxon and Mercian army on their way back to Northumbria. The Battle of Tettenhall followed, which the Danes lost. According to the *Anglo-Saxon Chronicle*, they lost thousands of men and two or three kings. This battle is also known as the last conflict between the Saxon army and the raiding Danes, who ravaged the English lands south of the River Humber.

After dealing with the Northumbrian Vikings, Edward was now free to concentrate his efforts on the southern Vikings, those who inhabited East Anglia and eastern Mercia. There, the Danes had founded five boroughs or main cities: Derby, Leicester, Lincoln, Nottingham, and Stamford. Each of these five boroughs was ruled by a Danish jarl (earl), but his lands around the cities were those that were used for the production of food.

Ethelred of Mercia died in 911, and his lands were ruled by his wife, Edward's sister Ethelfled. Together with his sister, Edward started building and repairing already existing fortresses around Mercia, not just to guard their lands but also to provide a base for the reconquest of eastern Mercia. After the territory was successfully taken, the fortresses served as defenses. One such fortress Edward ordered to be built was in Hertford in 912. This fortress served as the defense of London. Another one was built in Witham and yet another one in Maldon, Essex. Many people in Essex felt encouraged to bow to Edward's rule, even though they had lived in territories ruled by the Danes.

In 914, an army of Vikings from Brittany attacked the estuary of the River Severn. After ravaging the lands there, they moved toward Ergyng (Archenfield in Herefordshire), where they captured Bishop Cameleac. Edward was willing to pay a large sum for the ransom of this bishop; although it is not known why this man was so important to Edward, he paid forty pounds of silver just to free the bishop. The next year, this army of Vikings was defeated by the forces of Hereford and Gloucester. After this defeat, they released their hostages and promised they would leave these territories and never return. However, Edward was aware that the Danes often broke their oaths, and he kept an army at the Severn Estuary just in case. He was right, as the Vikings tried to attack these lands again on two separate occasions. Unable to progress, they turned their attention to Ireland.

The Severn Estuary and the territories of Ergyng are in southeastern Wales, and Edward's meddling in the Viking attacks there suggests Wales was under Wessex rule by 914.

917 was the decisive year in the war against the Danes. To defend his territories from the Vikings of Northampton, Edward constructed two new fortresses, one in Towcester and the other one in an unknown place, which is recorded only as Wigingamere. During the previous year, he reinforced the fortress of Bedford when Earl Thurketil, a Danish leader, submitted to the king of Wessex. The Vikings launched an attack on all three of these fortresses but were unsuccessful in capturing them. At the same time, Ethelfled led her army to Derby, which they managed to conquer. Both events are proof that the English system of defensive fortresses was a success.

The Danes tried to imitate the Anglo-Saxons, and they constructed their own fortresses. However, there was already much disunity and lack of coordination in the ranks of the Vikings. Their fortress at Tempsford in Bedfordshire was easily stormed by the Anglo-Saxons, and the last Danish king of East Anglia, Guthrum II, lost his life there in 918. The Wessex army proceeded to take Colchester, but they never even tried to hold it. They probably didn't need this town, though, as the existing fortresses proved to be defense enough. The Danes tried to retaliate for their dead king, but Edward easily won the victory at Maldon Fort. He then returned to Tempsford to reinforce the Danish fortress with a stone wall, after which the Northampton Vikings agreed to submit to him. Soon, the armies of Cambridge and East Anglia followed, and until the end of 918, the Danish forces that resisted were in four out of five boroughs: Leicester, Stamford, Nottingham, and Lincoln.

The first to fall was Leicester, which submitted to Edward's sister Ethelfled in 918 without any resistance. The Danes of Northumbria, who had been peaceful since 910, needed Mercian protection from the raiding Norwegians who came from Ireland. They were willing to swear allegiance to Ethelfled in return for protection, but she died on

June 12th, 918, and she never accepted the proposal. The Northumbrians never offered the same allegiance to her brother Edward, and so, Northumbrian York fell under the rule of the Norwegians in 919.

The *Anglo-Saxon Chronicle* records that after the death of Ethelfled, the Mercians submitted to King Edward. However, the Mercian version of the *Chronicle* has a different story to tell. After Ethelfled's death, her daughter, Elfwynn (Ælfwynn), took her title and became the Lady of the Mercians in December 918. But soon, her uncle deprived her of all authority, and she was taken to Wessex. Nothing else is known about Elfwynn as history never mentions her again. Edward suppressed the Mercian tendency for independence and submitted it to his rule completely.

Stamford also submitted without a fight to Edward before Ethelfled's death, and afterward, Nottingham did the same. The *Chronicle* describes that all the people who inhabited Mercia, both English and Danish, submitted to Edward by the end of 918. Some of the Danish jarls were allowed to keep their lands, but others were deprived of their possessions in order for King Edward to reward his most loyal people. Some territories and estates Edward kept for himself as his private property. By 919, Edward expanded his rule to all the lands south of the River Humber, and it seems only Northumbria still resisted the unification of the whole of England. But that would soon change when Edward's son, Athelstan, took the throne after his father's death.

Edward was first recorded with the nickname "the Elder" in the 10th century in the *Life of St. Aethelwold* by Wulfstan the Cantor, who was a monk in the Old Minster of Winchester. He used this nickname to distinguish King Edward of Wessex from Edward the Martyr, who had ruled East Anglia. Edward the Elder died at the royal estate of Farndon, situated south of Chester, on July 17th, 924. The cause of death is unknown, but it could be that he died of a wound sustained during a Mercian revolt that took place later in his life. He was buried in the New Minster of Winchester, but in 1110, his remains were transferred to the new church of Hyde Abbey, just outside the city walls of Winchester.

Chapter 10 – Athelstan (r. 924–927 and 927–939)

Athelstan succeeded the throne after his father's death in 924, and as the king of the Anglo-Saxons, he ruled until 927. He became the first king of England in 927, and he ruled from 927 to 939 with that title. However, he didn't inherit the throne without some dynastic trouble. When Edward the Elder died after the uprising in Mercia, Athelstan was with him, and the Mercians accepted him as the new king. However, his half-brother Elfweard (Ælfweard) ranked higher in their father's charters, and it seems Edward might have had the intention of proclaiming Elfweard as the successor to the throne of Wessex. It is possible that Edward disposed of Elfwynn, his sister's daughter who was the Lady of the Mercians, just so he could set Athelstan as the king of her territories. Although there is no hard evidence, it seems that Edward intended to divide his kingdom and set both of his sons as rulers.

While Athelstan was accepted as the king in Mercia, Wessex probably chose his half-brother Elfweard. However, he only lived sixteen days after Edward's death. The cause of death is not known. Even though Wessex had no ruler, it seems that Athelstan still had some difficulties being proclaimed king, as his coronation was delayed until September 925. The circumstances of his succession to the throne are uncertain, but some scholars suggest Athelstan agreed to not marry or have children so that after his death, the throne would pass to his younger half-brothers. Other historians propose that Athelstan's choice to not marry came from his religious views and aspiration to a purer life. Athelstan was finally crowned in the symbolic border area between Mercia and Wessex, known as Kingston upon the Thames, on September 4th, 925.

It seems that the center of Athelstan's opposition was in Winchester, and it continued to exist there even after he was crowned. There was animosity between the king and the bishop of Winchester, Frithestan, who refused to attend the coronation ceremony. He was also never mentioned as a witness to Athelstan's charters until 928, and even then, he was listed in a low position that didn't suit his senior rank. One of the Winchester nobles, Alfred, plotted to blind Athelstan to make him inadequate to rule, but he failed. It is uncertain if Alfred acted in support of Athelstan's half-brother Edwin or if he was trying to make himself a king. It is possible that the opposition in Winchester continued to exist until 933, which was when Athelstan's half-brother Edwin died in a shipwreck. His body was taken to his cousin in Boulogne, where it was buried at the Abbey of Saint Bertin. Historians believe Edwin was running England after the unsuccessful rebellion against the rule of his brother when he died. Thus, it was probably only then that the opposition in Winchester ceased to exist.

Athelstan's grandfather, Alfred the Great, held a ceremony when Athelstan was born and honored him with a scarlet cloak, a belt decorated with gems, and a sword in a gilded scabbard. Some medieval and modern scholars believe Alfred was designating Athelstan as a potential heir, as, at the time, the king of Wessex faced a dynastic rivalry with his nephew Ethelwold. Others believe Alfred was in an argument with his own son, Edward the Elder, and that he chose his grandson Athelstan as his heir instead of Edward. There is a third theory that believes Alfred intended to divide his kingdom between his son and grandson upon his death.

Alfred was also the one responsible for sending Athelstan to the Mercian court to be educated, where his aunt and uncle, Ethelfled and Ethelred, ruled. There, Athelstan gained military training as well, which would later enable him to conquer the remaining lands of the Danelaw and impose his rule over the whole of England. It is quite possible that Athelstan remained in Mercia when his father became the king of the Anglo-Saxons as a representative of his father's interests.

When Alfred died, Athelstan's father, Edward the Elder, married Elfflaed, his second wife. It is not known if Athelstan's mother had died or if she was put aside since a new political alliance had to be made. Nevertheless, Athelstan's position was weakened due to this new marriage, as Elfflaed favored her own children as the successors to the throne. Edward had two sons with his second wife, Elfweard and Edwin, but in 920, he married for the third time, putting Elfflaed aside. His third wife, Eadgifu, also had two sons, who would later become kings. Since Athelstan never married and never had children of his own, the throne eventually passed to his half-brothers, Edmund I and Eadred, respectively.

The King of the English

The Viking king of Northumbria, Sitric Cáech, had ruled from York since 920 when he crossed the sea from Ireland to inherit the throne of his kinsman Ragnall. Even though Ragnall submitted to the Anglo-Saxon king Edward the Elder, Sitric made it quite clear that he wouldn't follow in the footsteps of his predecessor when he raided Davenport in Cheshire, which was an obvious violation of the agreement between the two nations. Nothing else is known about Sitric until Edward the Elder died in 924. However, it seems that Sitric did rule a portion of land south of the River Humber, as his coins were found in the area. These coins contradict the *Anglo-Saxon Chronicle*, which states that no Viking came south of the

Humber after they submitted to Edward in 918. It is quite possible that the Vikings, under the leadership of Sitric, managed to reconquer a large area of Mercian land anywhere between 921 and 924 and that this event was unmarked by the *Chronicle*.

In 926, Athelstan met Sitric at Tamworth, where the king's sister married the Viking king of Northumbria. The two kings also made an agreement to never invade each other's territories or help each other's enemies. It was necessary for Sitric to convert to Christianity to be able to marry a Christian princess, but soon after, he reverted back to paganism. Only one year after his marriage, Sitric died of an unknown cause. He was succeeded by his cousin Guthfrith of Ivar, who was in Dublin at the time. However, before Guthfrith could arrive, Athelstan took the opportunity to invade Northumbria and seize the throne for himself. Guthfrith set sail from Dublin and tried to defend his right of inheritance, but Athelstan's army was stronger, and he easily won.

Even though Athelstan received the submission of the Danes who inhabited Northumbria, unrest followed, as they didn't want to be ruled by a southern king. The resistance to the southern rule only lasted for one year, and on July 12th, 927, King Athelstan received submission from not only Northumbria but also from King Constantine II of Alba (Scotland), King Hywel Dda of Deheubarth (South Wales), and Ealdred I of Bamburgh (former kingdom of Bernicia in northern Northumbria). There was one other king that submitted, but it remains unclear if this king was Owain of Strathclyde (southern Scotland) or Morgan ap Owain of Gwent (southeastern Wales). This event was followed by seven years of peace in the north of Britain.

Athelstan wasn't just the king of all the Anglo-Saxon people like his father. With the submission of the kingdoms of Wales and Scotland, Athelstan became the king and overlord of Britain. Many historians see his rule as the beginning of the imperial phase in England's history, which lasted between 925 and 975. Welsh sub-kings attended Athelstan's court and witnessed his charters. In fact, they were signed with a higher status than any other king or noble. It might be that Athelstan honored the Welsh rulers to justify the high taxes he imposed on their lands. For this, many Welshmen would come to resent the Saxon rule, and they even constructed a poem, "Armes Prydein Vawr" ("The Great Prophecy of Britain"), in which it is prophesied that the British would rise against their Saxon overlords and drive them into the sea.

A Problem in the North

Athelstan's position in the north was more delicate than when it came to Wales. The Scots never wanted the rule of the southern Saxon king, and Athelstan had trouble keeping his authority in their territories. The Scots always preferred to ally themselves with the pagan Vikings of Ireland, even though they accepted Christianity long ago. This means that Athelstan had to improve his position in the north in order to not lose it completely. The opportunity presented itself in 933 when his brother Edwin died and ended the Winchester opposition. The next year, Guthfrith, the king of Dublin, died, and the insecurity among the Danes started. They were in no position to send help to their allies in Scotland. For Athelstan, though, this meant the time was right to invade the north and impose his authority.

Athelstan's invasion of Scotland is briefly mentioned in the *Anglo-Saxon Chronicle* without much explanation. But the 12th-century chronicler John of Worcester claimed that King Constantine II of Scotland broke his treaty with Athelstan in 934; however, he doesn't mention the details of the treaty. Athelstan set out on a campaign in May of the same year, and with him were four Welsh kings, Hywel Dda of Deheubarth, Idwal Foel of Gwynedd, Morgan ap Owain of Gwent, and Tewdwr ap Griffri of Brycheiniog. The army was also accompanied by thirteen earls and their men, as well as eighteen bishops. Some of the earls were Danish men from East Anglia who joined their forces with the English navy instead of the ground forces.

No battles of this invasion of Scotland were recorded, and the outcome is not mentioned in any of the surviving sources. However, Simeon of Durham, in a chronicle from the 12th century, claims that the land army of Athelstan ravaged the lands as far as Dunnottar in northeastern Scotland, while the fleet raided Caithness and probably Orkney as well. Even though the outcome of the invasion is not recorded, it is clear that Athelstan managed to secure his authority over the north, as King Constantine II started signing his charters as a sub-king as early as September the same year.

However, this peace in the north only lasted for a few years. In 937, Constantine allied himself with Olaf Guthfrithson of Dublin, who had inherited the throne there and wanted to claim Northumbria as well. Backed by the Britons of the Kingdom of Strathclyde and their king, Owain, Constantine and Olaf led the attack, which was supposed to free them from the dominance of Wessex. Athelstan was surprised by their assault, as it occurred during the autumn. Typically, military campaigns in the medieval period took place during the summer. Athelstan couldn't assemble his army quickly enough, and the allies of Constantine plundered the English territories. The Welsh refused to join the West Saxon and Mercian armies, but they didn't support their British comrades either.

The main conflict between Athelstan and the alliance was the Battle of Brunanburh, which Athelstan won, preserving the unity of England. He had help from his younger half-brother Edmund, who would one day become king. Olaf was forced to return to Dublin, and Constantine returned to Scotland after losing his son in the battle. What happened to the king of Strathclyde, Owain, is not mentioned. The battle is recorded in the *Anglo-Saxon Chronicle* in the form of a praise poem called the "Battle of Brunanburh," which states that after the fighting, Athelstan and the Anglo-Saxon army pursued and slew many of their enemies. Even though Athelstan won and managed to preserve the unity of his kingdom, it seems that the resentment in the north only grew after this battle. When Athelstan died, Olaf came back from Ireland, and he managed to take Northumbria without any resistance, which shows that the people there were still reluctant to follow the southern Saxon leader.

Kingship

Athelstan ruled a wide kingdom, and he needed a modern administrative system in order to effectively govern all of its territories. As the first king of such a vast kingdom, he had to be innovative. Athelstan built a new administrative system on top of those of his predecessors, and the result was the most centralized government in the history of England. Athelstan kept the system of ealdormen, who ruled the shires and whose authority was just below the kings, in place. However, he expanded the areas that the earls controlled in order to reduce the number of ealdormen needed.

Right beneath the ealdormen were the royal officials known as reeves. This office was given to the local nobles and landowners, and they were in charge of the towns or royal estates. Medieval England wasn't a secular kingdom, and so, the Church worked together with the lay officials. The bishops and local abbots also attended the royal councils together with the nobles.

The royal council (known as the Witan) was the key mechanism of the English government. The place of the council meeting often changed, as the medieval courts did not have a permanent location. The king, his royal family, and their whole household would change locations throughout the kingdom in order to deal with arising crises. However, Athelstan mainly kept to Wessex and was reluctant to leave its borders. To deal with the problems of territories outside of Wessex, he would summon the ealdormen and nobles who were in charge there to come to him. Previous royal councils were small and intimate meetings between kings and their ealdormen. However, after the unification of England, a need for a much larger gathering of the prominent figures of the kingdom arose. Now, the royal council was attended not just by the local lords but also by the representatives of faraway territories, including bishops, thegns, and the kings who submitted to Athelstan's rule. Some historians even see these centralized royal councils as the predecessors of the Parliament of England.

In the area of law, there are many documents from Athelstan's time that have survived; in fact, more have survived from Athelstan's reign than any other 10th-century ruler. The first one seems to be the tithe edict and the "Ordinance on Charities." Scholars believe that the church officials had much to do with the writing of these laws, and it serves as evidence that the Church had an increased influence over the state during this period in history. Athelstan wrote that he was advised by the archbishop of Canterbury, Wulfhelm, and his bishops when he was writing this edict and the ordinance. The edict states the importance of paying tithes to the Church, while the ordinance regulates and enforces charity on the kingdom's reeves. The ordinance specifies the exact amount that needed to be given to the poor and also states that one slave needed to be freed annually.

As for secular laws, Athelstan considered stealing to be the greatest threat to the social order. He issued a law in which harsh penalties for thieving were introduced. Among them was even the death penalty for those who were above twelve. However, in later writings, Athelstan admitted these harsh measures didn't help much and that thieving continued to be one of the most frequent crimes in his kingdom. Desperate, he tried another strategy. Athelstan offered amnesty to the thieves who agreed to pay compensation to their victims. However, the problem of wealthy families protecting their relatives who were caught in the crime remained. One of the strategies to fight this problem was to send the criminals away from their families, often to the most distant parts of the kingdom. When the new measures didn't help either, Athelstan restored the old harsh penalties; however, he raised the age for the death penalty from twelve to fifteen, as he was concerned about how many young people were lost due to this law.

Athelstan inherited a love for learning from his grandfather Alfred the Great. Since ecclesiastical scholarship had declined during his father's reign, Athelstan was determined to reestablish its value and invest in monasteries that promoted learning. However, unlike his grandfather, Athelstan didn't care much about the general education of the people and saw the Church as the main center of education. He was extremely religious, and he often commissioned sacred manuscripts to be produced as gifts for various churches. Athelstan elevated ecclesiastical learning by bringing some of the most prominent scholars to England, among them being Israel the Grammarian, one of the most famous European scholars. He was a philosopher and a poet, but he was also the creator of a board game called "Gospel Dice," a game with a Christian spiritual concept. This game was often played at Athelstan's court, and from there, it spread around the kingdom.

Athelstan's court was where the hermeneutic style of Latin writing was revived. This style is known for its unusual use of archaic words, with the most popular words almost always derived from Greek. Many of Athelstan's charters were written in hermeneutic Latin, and the foreign scholars of his court were the most skilled practitioners of this style. Hermeneutic Latin even influenced the architecture of Athelstan's kingdom, as the builders sought to produce elaborate and enigmatic decorations for their constructions. Historians often connect this artistic style with Athelstan's ambition to show how his kingdom was successful and intellectual.

To be able to bring scholars from around Europe to work in his kingdom, Athelstan had to work hard on his relationships with the continental kingdoms. He also needed to devote special attention to the trade agreements and alliances he was making with prominent European kings. With the Carolingians, Athelstan maintained the good relations that had lasted for generations, considering his great-grandfather Ethelwulf married the Frankish princess Judith. Athelstan married one of his half-sisters, Eadgifu, to Charles the

Simple, the king of the West Franks, in 919. After Charles lost his kingdom, Eadgifu sent their son Louis to her brother's court as a protégé. Later, in 936, Athelstan helped Louis regain the throne of West Francia. However, Louis, who would become known as Louis IV, wasn't the only protégé of Athelstan. Having no children of his own, he gladly took in Alan II, Duke of Brittany, as his foster son. Like Louis, Alan was expelled from his lands, and in the same year he helped Louis, Athelstan helped Alan regain his ancestral possessions.

Luckily, Athelstan had many half-sisters who he could marry to foreign rulers in order to create alliances and good relations. Hugh the Great, Duke of the Franks, married Eadhild, but not before he sent many expensive gifts to Athelstan, such as the sword of Constantine the Great, a golden crown, and a piece of the crown of thorns that Jesus Christ wore when he was crucified. In East Francia, Athelstan also created family ties that would bind him to the kingdom, as he married his sister Eadgyth to Prince Otto of East Francia, who would later become King Otto I and eventually the Holy Roman emperor.

On October 27th, 939, Athelstan died at Gloucester. Even though all of his relatives and predecessors were buried at Winchester, Athelstan didn't want it as his burial place as it was the center of his opposition. Instead, he was buried at Malmesbury Abbey, where no other member of his family was ever buried. Unfortunately, Athelstan's remains were lost in the 16th century during the Reformation, but he was commemorated by an empty tomb made in his honor.

After his death, the united English kingdom fell apart, as the Danish Vikings immediately chose Olaf Guthfrithson of Dublin as the king in York. The north still remained a problem, and the Anglo-Saxon grasp over it collapsed soon after. Athelstan's successors, his half-brothers Edmund I and Eadred, respectively, were both devoted to restoring the united kingdom. Eadred was successful in 954 when the Northumbrians removed their Viking king Eric Bloodaxe and submitted to Anglo-Saxon rule. However, Wessex was no more. Even though it remained the center of the kingdom and the main dwelling choice of its kings, it was never independent again. Unlike Mercia, which continued to show its rebellious face until the Norman conquest, Wessex was transformed completely, as if it melted away and spread itself throughout the kingdom.

Conclusion

Wessex reemerged as an independent entity after the Danish conquest of England and the rule of the Danish King Cnut in 1016. He was the one who restored the old territories of Mercia, Northumbria, and East Anglia as earldoms, keeping Wessex for himself. After only a few years, Cnut made Wessex an earldom as well, and it consisted of all the English territories south of the Thames River. Those who were chosen to be ealdormen of Wessex were some of the richest and most powerful men of England, often right after the king. The first earl of Wessex was Godwin, the father of the future king of England and the last Anglo-Saxon king Harold Godwinson. In 1066, when Harold became the king, he returned Wessex to the Crown and chose not to give it as an earldom to any of his loyal nobles. This is why 1066 is often taken as the year when Wessex ceased to exist as a political entity.

However, Wessex continued to influence the culture of England, even after the Norman conquest; in fact, it influences culture even today. Its symbol, the dragon, or more accurately the wyvern, decorated the banners of Wessex armies in 752 when it was raised in the Battle of Burford. In the modern British Army, the 43rd Infantry Division, alternatively called the Wessex Division, adopted an emblem of a golden wyvern on a black or dark blue background. In the 1970s, the Wessex region got its own flag of a golden wyvern on a red field designed by William Crampton of the British Flag Institute.

Wessex remains a term that is used to describe the historical area that consists of Hampshire, the Isle of Wight, Dorset, Wiltshire, and parts of Berkshire and Somerset. As such, it continues to inspire modern authors whose imagination touches upon old medieval times. Through captivating stories and movies, we are still able to get a glimpse of its previous glory. It can be said that Wessex was the place of the birth of Britain. However, it is remembered far beyond the British Isles, as Wessex is a part of the Scandinavian sagas, which, in their own way, describe the Viking invasion of England.

Part 2: Mercia

A Captivating Guide to an Anglo-Saxon Kingdom of England and the Invasions of the Vikings during the 9th Century

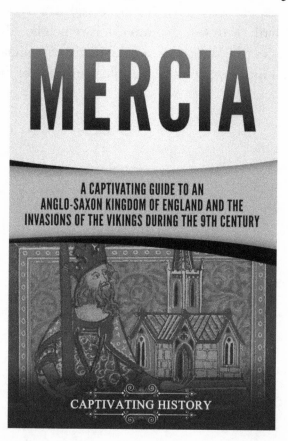

Introduction

The Kingdom of Mercia lasted for more than five hundred years. Such a long period of time brought change to all aspects of Mercian life, and it is the role of history and this book to follow that change through the centuries. But it wasn't just the kings and queens that changed. The events of the period resonated within social and cultural life, religious beliefs, artistic expression, and trade. Everything evolved under the patronage of Mercia.

We are able to understand these changes as they are still ongoing in modern times. The world we are living in is constantly shifting and developing, and as people, we are no different than the Anglo-Saxons from the old times. As such, it is no wonder we show interest in their way of life and the persons who ruled them. In fact, it is almost as if we feel a deep connection with the society of our ancestors, as if we feel there is some familiarity. The distance that separates our time from theirs is what makes this familiarity even more interesting.

The story of Mercia begins in the late 5th or early 6th century with the incursions of the Germanic tribes into the territories of the Midlands of England. It took almost a full century to form the first Kingdom of Mercia, which had well-defined borders and occupied the geopolitical territory of the Midlands. It wasn't long until Mercia became the obvious dominant force among all the Anglo-Saxon kingdoms, and it kept this status throughout the centuries. A series of strong leaders were born, and they extended the boundaries of the kingdom and made it more complex as time passed. The strong, independent kingdom allowed its people to develop an industry, to trade with other kingdoms and even nations, and to express themselves through religion and art.

What followed those blissful times of Mercian authority and dominance was a series of events that eventually led to its demise. Overrun by other, more powerful rulers, Mercia lost its independence but never its identity. Even as subjects to another crown, the Mercians distinguished themselves as a separate, rebellious people that yearned for their own independence and their own king or queen. However, time brings change, and as such, the will of the people shifts. Betrayed by his own people, the last earl of Mercia surrendered his territories, and they became integrated into the Kingdom of England. Still, Mercia continued to leave its own mark on England through language, culture, and art.

Timeline

410: Western Roman Emperor Honorius officially declares the cities of Britain need to take care of their own defenses. The end of direct Roman rule in Britain.

Late 4th century: The Anglo-Saxons launch their raids of Britain.

Circa 490: The Battle of Badon; Celtic British win against the Anglo-Saxons.

510–535: Icel leads his people across the North Sea to Britain.

628: Penda fights West Saxons at the Battle of Cirencester.

633: King Edward of Northumbria dies; Penda recognizes the overlordship of Oswald of Northumbria.

635 (Bede) or 641/2 (Welsh Chronicle): The Battle of Maserfield; King Penda frees Mercia from Northumbria and starts his rule as the first independent king of Mercia. Death of King Oswald of Northumbria.

655: Battle of Winwaed between Mercia and Bernicia; with Penda's death, Mercia became divided. Peada, Penda's son, rules southern Mercia.

658: Wulfhere, son of Penda, becomes the king of Mercia with Oswiu of Northumbria as overlord. Mercia becomes a Christian kingdom.

661: Wulfhere conquers West Saxons and Isle of Wight.

Circa 664: Wulfhere becomes the king of the East Saxons.

670: Oswiu of Northumbria dies; Ecgfrith becomes king of Northumbria.

674: Wulfhere attacks Northumbria but is defeated by Ecgfrith.

675: Wulfhere dies; Ethelred, third son of Penda, becomes king of Mercia.

676: Ethelred attacks Kent.

704: Ethelred abdicates the Mercian throne; Coenred, son of Wulfhere, becomes king.

709: Coenred abdicates in favor of Ceolred, Ethelred's son.

716: Ceolred dies, and the dynasty of Penda ends. Ethelbald, grandson of Penda's brother Eowa, becomes the king.

723: Ethelbald supports the succession of Ethelheard of Wessex.

733: Mercia and Wessex are at war.

740: Ethelheard of Wessex dies. Cuthred takes the throne of Wessex.

752: Cuthred attacks Mercia and frees Wessex from Mercian overlordship.

757: The assassination of Ethelbald; Beornred takes the throne of Mercia.

757: Offa defeats Beornred and takes Mercia.

760: Battle of Hereford between Mercia and Wales. Wales regains independence.

778/784/796: Renewed conflicts with Wales and building of Offa's dyke.

762: Ethelberht II of Kent dies; Offa takes overlordship of Kent.

776: Battle of Otford between Mercia and Kent; Kent regains independence.

779: Offa defeats Wessex and becomes its overlord.

780s: Charlemagne proposes a marriage between his son and Offa's daughter. Offa offends Charlemagne, who bans English traders to enter French harbors.

785/6: Offa takes Kent as its sole ruler.

790: Offa gains overlordship over Sussex and East Anglia.

793: The first Viking raid in Britain at the monastery of Lindisfarne.

Circa 796: Charlemagne makes peace with Offa; trade is renewed.

796: Offa dies; Coenwulf becomes the king of Mercia.

798: Mercia defeats Kent.

798: Mercia invades Wales.

801: Coenwulf gives the rule of Kent to his brother Cuthred.

802: Ecgberht becomes king of Wessex, which regains its independence.

807: Cuthred dies; Coenwulf takes the rule of Kent.

821: Coenwulf dies; Ceolwulf I becomes king. The decline of Mercia starts.

823: Beornwulf disposes of Ceolwulf and takes the throne of Mercia.

825: The Battle of Ellandun against Wessex, in which Mercia loses.

826: Beornwulf dies and is succeeded by Ludeca.

827: Ludeca is killed; Wiglaf takes the throne of Mercia.

829: Wiglaf loses Mercia; Ecgberht of Wessex rules Mercia for a year.

830: Wiglaf takes back Mercia.

839: Wiglaf dies; Beorhtwulf becomes king of Mercia.

841: The Vikings attack London.

851: The Vikings repeat the attack on London. Beorhtwulf probably dies at this point.

852: Burgred becomes king of Mercia.

865: The Great Heathen Army invades Britain.

866: The Vikings conquer York.

867: The Vikings invade Mercia and take Nottingham.

871: Alfred the Great becomes king of Wessex.

874: Burgred is expelled from Mercia by the Vikings. Ivar the Boneless dies; Guthrum becomes leader of the Vikings. Ceolwulf II becomes king of Mercia as a puppet king for the Vikings.

877: Ceolwulf surrenders part of Mercia to Guthrum.

878: The Vikings attack Wessex; Alfred escapes the Vikings. Later in the year, Alfred wins a battle against the Vikings, and the Treaty of Wedmore comes into effect. Guthrum accepts Christianity and takes the name Ethelstan. The treaty also defines the borders of the Danelaw, and Mercia as a kingdom ceases to exist.

879/880: Ceolwulf II of Mercia deposed; Alfred rules Mercia directly.

888: Guthrum (Christian name Ethelstan) dies.

892: The Vikings attack Wessex.

899: Alfred the Great dies; Edward the Elder becomes king of Wessex.

917: The Vikings attempt invasion of Mercia but lose the Battle of Derby.

918: Ethelfled, Lady of the Mercians, dies; the Mercians submit to Edward the Elder of Wessex.

924: The Mercians rebel against the rule of King Edward the Elder, but he quells the rebellion. Edward dies in the same year. Ethelstan, son of Edward the Elder, becomes king of the Anglo-Saxons.

Chapter 1 – The Origins of Mercia

Mercia and the surrounding kingdoms

(https://upload.wikimedia.org/wikipedia/commons/thumb/0/0b/ England_green_top.svg/800px-England_green_top.svg.png)

To ask questions about the origins of Mercia is to seek an answer that tells the story of all Anglo-Saxon kingdoms.

Mercia was a part of what we today call the Anglo-Saxon Heptarchy. This was a collection of seven kingdoms that were later united under the Kingdom of England. East Anglia, Essex, Kent,

Mercia, Northumbria, Sussex, and Wessex were all kingdoms ruled by the Anglo-Saxons, and they were all a part of the Heptarchy. However, one must be very careful when naming these kingdoms. They were never stable kingdoms with well-defined borders, as there were many fluctuations over time. "Sub-kingdoms" were formed and lost, and lands were often divided or united to build supremacy in various regions. These kingdoms, even though not well-defined, never actually numbered seven. But the regions, to which we refer today when we speak of Anglo-Saxon rule, are seven. This is why the term "Heptarchy" is in use.

The first time the seven kingdoms were mentioned as such was in the 12th century in *Historia Anglorum* ("History of the English"), written by Henry of Huntingdon. The division of Anglo-Saxon kingdoms is not a modern construction—it existed even in the Middle Ages. But the Anglo-Saxon kingdoms themselves are much older than that. Their history starts in the period known as the Dark Ages or the Early Middle Ages, and it is tied to the end of Roman Britain in the 5th century.

The Transition

During the reign of Emperor Honorius (r. 393–423), the decline of the Western Roman Empire was very much obvious, and it happened in a short period of time. In 410, the emperor declared that the cities, then called *civitates*, of Britain had to take care of their own defenses. However, it was even before this official declaration that the Roman forces were denuded or moved out of the British Isles. With the army leaving Britain, many administrative workers and even civilians felt the urge to move away in search of new prospects. The Roman Empire was obviously abandoning this region, and so, the people moved away, following the empire's withdrawal. But it wasn't only the military and the civilians of the Roman Empire that started moving. The citizens of Britain had to migrate and resettle as well, moving from the abandoned cities and settlements to the ones that survived and offered some kind of certainty. This period of Britain's history is known as the "barbarian migration," and it is this period that gave birth to so many myths and legends about the origin of the Anglo-Saxon kingdoms. It was also during this migration period that the Anglo-Saxon tribes came to Britain.

Even though the coming of the Anglo-Saxon tribes to the territories of Britain is seen as an invasion, and it is often called the "Anglo-Saxon Invasion," it was more of a process and migration of peoples that took time. The term invasion suggests one event, probably hostile in nature, that managed to change the cultural image of Britain from Roman to Germanic. And indeed, old sources often talk about the hostilities between the Anglo-Saxons and the local population. However, a more probable modern view of the Anglo-Saxon settlement in Britain is that their migration was not a large-scale one. It was more oriented toward the warrior caste, who came to Britain as mercenaries and stayed. They managed to rise up in ranks and impose their own dominance over the local peoples. When the numbers of Anglo-Saxon elite rose, only then were they able to unite under one national identity and impose their own political and social values on the peoples of Britain, who still dwelled in its Roman past. It was these first Anglo-Saxon leaders who invited even more Germanic tribes to come and settle in Britain.

The origin of these Germanic tribes can be placed today in the regions of Germany, the Netherlands, and Denmark. Some tribes were welcomed in the lands where their Saxon ancestors established rule, but others had to fight for their right to settle and live in the new lands. The encounters with the domestic peoples were often hostile and bloody, and this is where the myth of the great invasion and genocide comes from. However, the percentage of Anglo-Saxon individuals in the 6th century was barely 5 percent, which indicates that the Germanic tribes never committed genocide on a large scale and had no intention of replacing the existing population of Britain. Instead, what they managed to do was impose their dominion and convert the people. Many native lords were pressured into declaring themselves Anglo-Saxon after military losses.

The Britons did try to resist Anglo-Saxon settlement, and one figure among them rose to prominence. It is in the early texts of Gildas the Wise, a monk from the 6th century, where Ambrosius Aurelianus is mentioned for the first time. He was the last Romanized ruler or overlord of Britain who fought against Anglo-Saxon settlement on the island. Many myths surround the persona of Ambrosius, and it is hard to discern where he comes from and how he rose to power. Some myths go so far as to call him the uncle of the legendary King Arthur, while others mention him in the role of Merlin the wizard. But Gildas tells us that Ambrosius fought the Anglo-Saxons for ten years, which pushes us to assume that he was the leader of the British forces in the Battle of Badon in circa 490.

It is believed that this great battle was a resistance effort to repel the Anglo-Saxon invaders, but there are no documents that associate Ambrosius directly with this battle. Nevertheless, what we can conclude from the mention of Ambrosius and his resistance is that the Anglo-Saxons and the Britons did not mix at first. It took almost three generations for the Germanic tribes to start intermingling with the natives, intermarrying and imposing their culture.

Only at the end of the 6th century did the Anglo-Saxons start forming their own settlements, which would come to dominate certain regions, and it was these regions that came to be the Anglo-Saxon kingdoms. However, Mercia didn't exist in this early Anglo-Saxon history. There was no unified administrative entity in the territories of the English Midlands. The evolution of these lands from the Welsh Marches, with sparse settlements, to the Kingdom of Mercia is obscure, and it relies heavily on the mythical beliefs of the land.

Mercia Foundation Legends

The *Anglian collection*, a manuscript that lists all the kings of England, mentions Penda as the first ruler of Mercia, who started his reign in the 7th century. However, Anglo-Saxon royal genealogies go much earlier in time and speak of Icel, a semi-legendary leader from the migration times, who is said to be a direct descendant of Woden (Odin). Another mention of Icel as the first leader of the people of Mercia is found in a text from the 8th century written by an East Anglian monk named Felix, *Vita S. Guthlaci.* Saint Guthlac was the son of a Mercian noble named Penwalh, who claimed he could trace his origins all the way back to Icel, who founded the dynasty named after him, the Iclingas, who ruled Mercia.

Icel, in turn, was the great-grandson of Offa of Angel, a legendary king of the Angles who is mentioned in the Old English poem "Widsith" from the 8th century. The more important mention of Offa is in *Beowulf,* but it is unknown if it is the same person. Later kings of Mercia were eager to affiliate themselves with the heroes of this epic poem, often claiming this Offa to be their forefather. King Offa of Mercia, who ruled from 757 to 796, may have deliberately compared himself to the legendary Offa from *Beowulf,* drawing a parallel between some of his deeds with the deeds of the hero. For example, *Beowulf*'s Offa set a boundary at the River Eider that was to protect his people from the Saxon clan of Myrging. At the same time, King Offa built a famous dike that still stands at the current border of England and Wales. His intention was to protect his Mercian kingdom from the Welsh Kingdom of Powys.

However, there is a belief present among literary circles that it was King Offa or one of his descendants who deliberately spread the chapter about the hero Offa and his wife Thryth in the poem of *Beowulf.* The chapter itself seems to have no poetic purpose and is only a digression in *Beowulf.* Scholars believe the passage about Offa was added to the main body of the poem very clumsily, as it obviously stands out and has no direct links with the hero Beowulf. The purpose of the chapter was to compliment King Offa of Mercia and to connect him directly with the heroes of old times. If that was the case, one question must be asked: Why is the hero Offa's wife

Thryth presented as bloodthirsty and violent? It is obvious she is a depiction of Kings Offa's wife, Cynethryth of Mercia. Wouldn't she be depicted in a positive light as well in order to emphasize the true and just rule of her husband? Scholars offer us satisfactory answers to the violence that surrounds her character. The story of Thryth is used to confirm the blame of Cynethryth, who is believed to have been directly involved in the assassination of King Ethelbert (Æthelberht) II of East Anglia, even though it was King Offa who issued the order. Another name that appears in *Beowulf* is Eomer, the grandson of Offa and father to Icel, the founder of the Mercian dynasty.

It wasn't only the heroes of old that Mercian kings liked to affiliate themselves with. They also claimed a divine descent through family ties with no less than Woden (Odin) himself. This claim was made by all Anglo-Saxon kings, and it can be seen by the Anglo-Saxon genealogies, which shows how all royal dynasties lead back to Woden. But what stays unclear to history is whether the Anglo-Saxons who migrated to Britain actually saw Woden as a god or if he was a heroic figure who went through euhemerism (the idea that myths may originate from real actions and people) to become a god. It is believed that the Anglo-Saxons thought of Woden as a hero, whose stories were overexaggerated into myths and legends. However, a recent discovery of a bracteate, a medallion worn in northern Europe during the migration period, which depicts Woden as a deity, questions the theory of him being just a hero. It would certainly be beneficial to connect a dynasty to a deity, and it comes as no surprise why the kings of Mercia, as well as other Anglo-Saxon kings, claimed they were the descendants of a god or hero even during the rise of Christianity. Royal genealogy often changed to suit the political stage of the time. It was used as a tool for propaganda, and as such, it required many famous names to be included, whether they were real notable people or the heroes of old poems and tales.

Table 1. Genealogy of the legendary Mercian rulers up until Pybba, the first recorded king of Mercia in *Historia Brittonum*.

Anglian collection	Anglo-Saxon Chronicle	Beowulf
Pybba	Pybba	
Crioda	Creoda	
Cynewald	Cynewald	
Cnebba	Cnebba	
Icil	Icel	
Eamer	Eomer	Eomer
Angengeot	Angelbeow	
Offa	Offa	Offa
Waermund	Waermund	Waermund
Wihtlaeg	Wihtlaeg	
Weodulgeot		
Woden	Woden	

The First Kings of Mercia

It is not known when Mercia was first regarded as a separate kingdom or how it came to be, and there are no written records that could give us a clue. What is known is that Mercia was the last kingdom to be Christianized, and this is possibly the reason for the lack of information about its earlier times. Today, we mostly rely on the Christian documents of priests, monks, kings, and the kingdoms of the Middle Ages. The Christianization of Britain started as early as the 3rd century CE. However, Mercia was converted only in the 7th century, leaving a big unrecorded gap in its history. But this doesn't mean historians can only guess at what happened in Mercia before its Christianization. There are records of Mercia in the documents of other kingdoms, and there are Mercian pagan archeological findings that give us an insight into what life was like in the kingdom during those times. The simplest way to reconstruct the earliest history of Mercia would be to look at what we know of its first rulers. This time, we should look away from the myths and legends, away from the heroes of *Beowulf* and "Widsith," and look at the records left behind by monks whose sole work was to write down history. One such document would be the *Historia ecclesiastica gentis Anglorum* ("Ecclesiastical History of the English People"), a famous work written by Bede the Venerable, a monk who lived during the 8th century. This document is the earliest work of history that focuses on Anglo-Saxon England. Since he was native to Northumbria, Bede emphasizes its importance in the medieval English world and offers a critical view of Mercia, Northumbria's southern rival kingdom. It is in this work that Bede notes the regal years of Penda as Mercia's first ruler. However, unlike the *Anglo-Saxon Chronicle*, Bede mentions an earlier king of Mercia by the name of Cearl. He speaks of a marriage between this Mercian king's daughter and Edwin of Deira, the ruler of the lands that would later become part of Northumbria.

There are historical texts that attempt to go much earlier in time before Penda, but they were written at a later date. For example, a

12th-century historian, Henry of Huntingdon, in his work, *Historia Anglorum*, claims that Creoda (or Crioda) was the founder of the Kingdom of Mercia in 585 when he began his rule. Henry goes further and tells how he was succeeded by Pybba, who ruled for only three years. The next in line was Cearl, who ruled for ten years until he was succeeded by Penda, who Bede and the *Anglo-Saxon Chronicle* mention as the first ruler of Mercia. Although some historians include the genealogy offered in *Historia Anglorum* in the list of Mercia's earliest kings, others are reluctant to do so as the manuscript does not offer the sources of information. Even though the *Anglo-Saxon Chronicle* offers the same names that appear in *Historia Anglorum*, the context of their appearance is much different. For example, Creoda is mentioned as a West Saxon, not Mercian.

The *Anglian collection*, an assemblage of four manuscripts of royal genealogies, starts their list of Mercian kings with Pybba (r. c. 593–606). However, *Historia Brittonum* ("The History of the Britons"), a compilation of historical texts from the 8th century, implies that during Pybba's time, Mercia was a part of Northumbria, and it was King Penda who freed the Kingdom of Mercia in 641 or 642 following the Battle of Maserfield. Other sources mention the same battle in another context. Bede talks about the Northumbrians fighting for supremacy over the territories of Britain south of the Humber estuary, and he paints a very biased illustration of King Oswald of Northumbria as an enlightened martyr.

The Annales Cambriae ("The Annals of Wales"), a historical document from the 12th century, speaks of two kings of Mercia, Penda and Eowa, who was possibly Penda's brother. In this context, Eowa was the dominant king of Mercia at the time, and with his death during the Battle of Maserfield, Penda was able to unite northern and southern Mercia under one king. There is a possibility that Eowa, who ruled over the northern parts of Mercia, was a subject to Oswald of Northumbria and that he fought as his ally against

Penda. In this context, if Penda wasn't the first king of Mercia, he can at least be seen as one of its most significant rulers, as he was the one who united the divided kingdom and set it on the stage of world politics in medieval times as an important player.

The Mercians

But who were the Mercians actually? What we know so far is that they came to Britain during the great migration, which followed the retreat of the Roman Empire from the British Isles. We also know the Mercians were made up of Germanic tribes that settled in the English Midlands and whose geopolitical borders were not strictly defined until the 7th century.

The name Mercia is the Latin form of the Old English word Merce (or Mierce/Myrce in the West Saxon dialect), and it is translated as "border people." The name suggests Mercia was a territory that represented a border of some kind, although it is still not clarified between which geographical regions. The traditional opinion is that Mercia stood as a border between the Welsh people and the Anglo-Saxon invaders. However, some academics propose an alternative interpretation. P. Hunter Blair, an Anglo-Saxon specialist, claims Mercia was the border between Northumbria and all the tribes of the Trent River valley. The divide, in his opinion, comes from the simple fact that historians are not sure who exactly the Mercians were. They settled in the Midlands during the times of the great migrations of people, an event that makes it almost impossible to discern the tribes and peoples that moved across the territory of the British Isles during this period. However, the answer might lie in linguistics and one particular Anglian tribe that shares the name with the first Mercian dynasty.

The traditional belief is that Mercians are the East Angles who eventually moved inland in the search for new land to cultivate. Upon settling in the English Midlands, this group became distinguished by the name of Middil Angles or Middle Angles. However, there is no historical document that will confirm this theory; we can only base this on oral tradition, which would be recorded at a much later date, and so, its trustworthiness should be doubted. However, an Anglian tribe that went under the name Iclingas painted the larger picture of these migrations.

The first Angles who arrived in the territory of today's Britain settled in the area known by the name Iceni, which would later be known as East Anglia. Linguists link the word Iceni to the tribal name Icel, attributing the ending "i" to the Romans and the suffix "n" to the plural form of the word. Therefore, it is quite possible that Icel wasn't the name of the first mythological king of the Mercians. In fact, it could be a tribal name whose meaning has been lost over time and which was later attached to the mythological hero whose purpose was to define and explain the national identity of the people who inhabited the Middle Angles. It was from this tribal name that the dynasty Icelingas/Iclingas got their name, probably since it was already known to their subjects as it defined their very existence in the territories of what would later become Mercia.

It was in the 7th century that Mercia became a defined kingdom. The Tribal Hidage from the same century gives us an insight into what the Mercian territories may have looked like in geographical terms. The Tribal Hidage is a list of Anglo-Saxon tribes and also details the measurement of the units of land, also known as a hide, that was in their possession. At the top of the list is Mercia with 30,000 hides, and it is believed it covered much of today's territories of Derbyshire, Leicestershire, Nottinghamshire, Northamptonshire, Staffordshire, and Warwickshire.

However, Bede writes it differently. According to him, in the year 655, after the Battle of the Winwaed in which Penda died, Mercia was again split into two divisions, with the north counting 7,000 and the south 5,000 hides. According to Bede, during the 7th century, Mercia did not have more than 12,000 hides in total. It could be that Bede was referring to the core kingdom, something we could call the "original Mercia," while the Tribal Hidage refers to all other tribes that were under Mercian rule. This would mean that Mercia had dominion over the neighboring tribes that are also listed separately in the Hidage. If this was the case, it could mean that the Mercians weren't just one tribe and that the term expanded to all the people who accepted the authority of the Mercian rulers. It is only natural for a ruling tribe to impose their dominion over its neighbors, and accepting Mercian authority might have given them the honor of calling themselves Mercians. But that doesn't mean they were all the same people.

Mercian authority fluctuated over the course of time due to the military successes of their kings, and so, Mercia could have gone from the initial 12,000 hides to 30,000 in a very short span of time. The borders of kingdoms were constantly changing, and it could have happened that one family could call themselves Mercian one day and Northumbrian the next. It all came down to where their tribute payments went, whether it was to the Mercian or Northumbrian kings. The origin of the people did not matter, as Bede himself said in his *Historia ecclesiastica* that the people were ruled by the king, and it was the king's origin that mattered. If the king was Mercian, the people he ruled were Mercians as well, whether they were born in the kingdom or became Mercian by conquest.

Chapter 2 – The Builders of Mercia

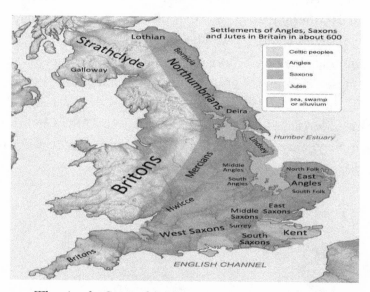

The Anglo-Saxon kingdoms around the year 600

https://upload.wikimedia.org/wikipedia/commons/thumb
/e/ee/Britain_peoples_circa_600.svg/800px-Britain_peoples_circa_600.svg.png

The Kingdom of Mercia was built on the supreme political power of all Anglo-Saxon kingdoms. It was built by warlords whose successful military campaigns against their neighbors brought political and economic power during the Early Middle Ages. The first Mercian dynasty, the Icelingas, traced their lineage all the way to the heroes of old and to the divine Woden himself, but it was Penda and his brothers Eowa and Coenwealh who were the true representatives of the early Kingdom of Mercia. Later, kings always claimed they were direct descendants of Penda or of his brothers as if it was a symbol of prestige. Indeed, Penda was a political colossus of his time, as he dominated the history of England in the 7th century.

Bede gives us a list of seven *bretwaldas*, kings who achieved lordship over all or some of the Anglo-Saxon kingdoms. *Bretwalda* is an old English word, and its meaning is still being disputed as it can mean either "Britain-ruler" or "Wide-ruler." Even though Mercian kings are considered to have been the most powerful rulers in the Early Middle Ages, none of them had the honor to be titled *bretwalda* as both Bede's *Historia ecclesiastica* and the *Anglo-Saxon Chronicle* are anti-Mercian in nature. The Mercians were the last to undergo Christianization and were regarded as no more than uncivilized heathens by their contemporaries, no matter whether their power was the most dominant in the Anglo-Saxon world.

Penda (r. c. 626–655)

The most detailed source of Penda's life comes from Bede's *Historia ecclesiastica*, and since Bede was a Northumbrian, he was very biased in his observations of history. Penda was nothing more than a maker of Christian martyrs in Bede's eyes; however, he did acknowledge Penda's royal lineage, saying he was a man of the royal stock of the Mercians, gifted as a warrior. Other less reliable sources of Penda's life come from the *Anglo-Saxon Chronicle* and *Historia Brittonum*. However, both of these manuscripts are of a later date, and they do not offer the sources by which they were written.

Another interesting fact is the king's name, Penda. The Mercian king was the first to be mentioned carrying this name, and it seems he was the only one, as there was no other Penda ever recorded after his rule. However, there are few geographical places in the western

Midlands that are believed to be named after him, such as Pinnbury and Peddimore.

Penda became the king of Mercia in 626, according to *Historia Anglorum*, which was written in the 12ᵗʰ century. However, there is no description of the ways in which he assumed power. Penda was one of the many sons of Pybba, but it is unclear whether he was a direct successor to the throne or whether he gained the right to rule by conquest. Bede mentions Cearl as Penda's predecessor, which can either mean that they were kinsmen or rivals. The *Anglo-Saxon Chronicle*, a document from the 9ᵗʰ century, mentions the same year as the *Historia Anglorum* as the year of Penda's succession to the throne. It goes further to describe that he was fifty years old at the time and that he ruled for thirty years. However, the *Anglo-Saxon Chronicle* is confusing with the information it offers, as it says that Penda's sons were very young when he died. One of them, Wulfhere, was just an infant. This would mean that Penda, who was eighty when he died, was a father to an infant. This is something that modern historians observe with a grain of salt, considering the life expectancy during the Middle Ages and the likelihood of fathering a child at such an advanced age. What is more likely is that the *Anglo-Saxon Chronicle* meant to say that Penda ruled for thirty years but was fifty when he died. This would mean he assumed the throne at the age of twenty. This makes more sense considering the historical timeframe at which we are looking. Also, the *Anglo-Saxon Chronicle* is not preserved in its original writing. We only have its copies, which could have lost some of the original information during the process of transcribing.

Bede is generally seen as the most reliable source of information when it comes to the Early Middle Ages as he was a contemporary historian and scholar. This doesn't mean he wasn't biased, though. He was for sure writing in the service of Northumbrian propaganda, like many other royal scholars that were taken under a nobleman's patronage. However, Bede is the most likely to have the correct facts such as ages, years, and names. Bede describes Penda as "a most warlike man of the royal race of the Mercians" and that he ruled Mercia for 22 years after the defeat of King Edwin of Northumbria in 633. The language Bede uses leaves us wondering whether he meant to say that Penda was already the king of Mercia when Edwin of Northumbria died in 633 or that it was only after Edwin's death that Penda became the ruler.

It is safe to assume that Penda was a warlord of royal Mercian origins, not a king, before 633. He could have also been one of the rulers of the divided lands of Mercia, and it was only after the victory over Edwin of Northumbria, the most powerful king in Britain at the time, that Penda managed to unite the lands and rule them as their sole sovereign.

Penda's first mention in historical records is always in relation to the Battle of Cirencester in 628, where he fought the West Saxons, who were under the leadership of Kings Cynegils and Cwichelm. This is probably the reason some sources mention the year of this battle as the year when Penda's rule began. But it was more likely he was just a warlord at that time. As a result of Penda's efforts, the province of Hwicce, which lay in the southwestern Midlands, became a part of Mercia. The victory against the West Saxons must have brought Penda some prestige, as right after it, he joined forces with the British (Welsh) King Cadwallon of Gwynedd. But his role in the alliance was that of a vassal, which meant Penda did not have the same right to the victor's spoils. This is another reason modern historians believe he was just a warlord at the time and that he was trying to build a reputation for himself and find a place in the political scene of Britain. For Bede, this alliance was a terrible thing, as Cadwallon, a Christian king, made a deal with the pagan warlord Penda and the idol-worshiping Mercians.

It is believed that Cadwallon was mostly unsuccessful in repelling the Northumbrians, whose intention was to expand their kingdom in northern Britain. Northumbria was allied with East Anglia at first, but they lost their support, and Cadwallon saw the opportunity to strike at the weakened enemy. Penda joined Cadwallon, and together, they led their forces against Edwin of Northumbria. The battle took place in the marshy areas of Hatfield Chase, whose name it still bears, near today's Doncaster in South Yorkshire. Bede records the date of the battle as October 12th, 633, as this is the date when his king, Edward of Northumbria, died, together with his son and heir, Osfrith. His second son, Eadfrith, was captured by Penda and later killed. The Northumbrian kingdom, posing no threat of expanding to northern territories, was divided into Bernicia and Deira. This division of Northumbria lasted only for one year, as Oswald came to power and managed to kill Cadwallon at the Battle of Heavenfield, after which he united Northumbria once more. With these achievements, Oswald became the most powerful king in Britain and even deserved the title of *bretwalda*.

Penda was now forced to recognize the overlordship of Oswald, but the history is obscure when it comes to his actions during this time. He killed Edwin's son Eadfrith, who he had kept captive since the Battle of Hatfield Chase, probably due to a demand from Oswald, who saw the prince as a threat to his throne. Mercian historians of a later age note that Penda posed a considerable threat to the Northumbrians during those times and that Oswald could not attack such a mighty force, but this could be nothing more than an exaggeration coming from Penda's successors. If Penda was that mighty to be able to oppose Oswald, then there was no advantage to be gained by killing Eadfrith, Oswald's rival. Penda could have used him to divide Northumbria, weaken it, and then conquer it. However, there is also the possibility Penda had his own reasons to kill Edwin's son, who was indeed the grandson of Cearl, Penda's predecessor. This means that Eadfrith was a threat to both the royal dynasties of Northumbria and Mercia.

During the reign of King Oswald of Northumbria, Penda's attention was turned toward East Anglia and their king, Ecgric, whom he defeated. The year of this battle is uncertain, but historians place it at around the year 635. Bede describes how Penda warned Ecgric in order to allow him to gather an army and defend himself. Even Sigeberht, the former king of East Anglia and Ecgric's kinsman who had retired to the monastery of Beodricesworth (today's Bury of St. Edmunds), joined the battle, thinking his presence would motivate the army. It wasn't enough. Penda defeated the East Anglian army and killed both Ecgric and Sigeberht. Mercia spread its authority over East Anglia, and now, Penda posed a serious threat to Oswald, who had to react.

During the 630s, Penda probably ruled the southern part of Mercia, while the north was under his brother Eowa. However, there is no evidence that would suggest what kind of relations were between the two brothers. They could have ruled as co-rulers, or they could have been enemies. Some historians believe that Eowa was a king who ruled the northern parts but recognized Penda's kingship. However, co-ruling wasn't unusual during the early Anglo-Saxon kingdoms, and it is most likely that the brothers ruled their kingdoms respectively.

As Penda's influence over Britain grew, Oswald of Northumbria had to fight him. What exactly caused the Battle of Maserfield, which followed in 635, is unknown, but Penda and Oswald finally clashed. Bede reports the date of the battle to be August 5th, 635, but the Welsh document *Annales Cambriae* places the battle in 641. It is believed that Bede proposed the correct date since the Welsh document is of a later date and of unknown origin. Penda won in the Battle of Maserfield, and Oswald died. Bede tells us how Oswald's cause for the battle was just, which might mean Oswald was defending his own territories. However, the suggested place of the battle was well in his enemy's territory. The most likely location where the battle took place is today's Oswestry, a town whose name's etymology is "Oswald's Tree." The Welsh name of the same place is *Croesoswallt*, which translates to "Oswald's Cross" and supports the belief that Oswald's body was crucified after the battle. At the time of the battle, this place belonged to the Kingdom of Powys, which was Penda's Welsh ally. This would mean that Bede was wrong and that Oswald fought deep in enemy territory, which he would only do if he was leading an offensive campaign.

Some historians believe that this battle was a simple war between Christians and pagans. However, the presence of Christian Welshmen who fought on the pagans' side makes us wonder if this was true. It seems more probable that either Oswald tried to expand his kingdom or that he was trying to subdue Penda, whose influence in the region continued to grow. Whatever the reason for the battle was, it resulted in yet another division of Northumbria to its component kingdoms of Deira and Bernicia. On the other hand, Penda and Mercia rose as leaders in the region. Penda united Mercia after his brother Eowa died in the same battle. It is unclear on which side Eowa fought, though. There is a possibility that, as the ruler of northern Mercia, he recognized the overlordship of Northumbria and fought on its side against his own brother. Whatever the case may be, Penda became the most powerful Mercian leader that ever ruled the Midlands and the most formidable king in Britain. He managed to hold all this power until his death in 655.

Penda chose to exercise his power by continuously raiding Bernicia, which was now ruled by Oswiu, Oswald's brother. Oswiu avoided confronting Penda in an open battle for a long time, probably due to realizing his kingdom was much weaker than Mercia. Some historians even suggest that this feeling of weakness might have had a religious connotation. Penda was known as a warrior-king protected by pagan gods who were seen as more efficient in offering their support in warfare than the Christian God. However, there is evidence that suggests that Penda wasn't constantly hostile toward Bernicia, as his own daughter, Cyneburh, married Oswiu's son Alhfrith. Penda even married his son Peada to Oswiu's daughter, Alhflaed (Alhflæd). Peada ruled over the Middle Angles at that time, but to make the marriage with the Christian princess possible, he had to convert not just himself but his whole kingdom to Christianity. Bede said that at this point, Penda remained pagan, but he allowed the Christians to practice their religion in the Kingdom of Mercia. There are speculations that it was Oswiu who persuaded Peada to marry his daughter in order to turn him against his father with the purpose of weakening Mercia. This could have been the event that set the scene for the Battle of the Winwaed in 655, where Penda was defeated and killed.

Again, it was Bede who gives us the account of the Battle of the Winwaed, which he dates as happening on November 15th, 655. It is also said that this battle was probably the most important between the northern and southern Anglo-Saxon kingdoms of the Early Middle Ages, but very little is known about it. One of the possible reasons for the battle was Bernicia's sponsorship of Christianity in pagan Mercia. Although Penda tolerated Christian practices in his kingdom, he might have seen Bernicia's attempt of religious influence as a sign of possible religious colonialism. This would directly influence his power over Mercia, and Penda could not allow that to happen. Instead, he chose to initiate a war between the two kingdoms.

The armies met at the Winwaed, a river that has yet to be identified but is believed to have been one of the tributaries of the Humber. Penda entered the territories of Bernicia with thirty warlords and their men. These warlords were probably his allies from East Anglia and Wales, which included their rulers, Cadafael ap Cynfeddw of Gwynedd and Ethelhere (Æthelhere) of East Anglia. Penda was also supported by the king of Deira, Ethelwald (Æthelwald), Oswiu's nephew who clearly had no love for his uncle and who guided the Mercian army through Bernicia's territories. It is possible that Ethelwald, who was the son of Oswald of Northumbria, wanted to use Penda as a means by which to acquire Bernicia's throne for himself.

Bede isn't the only one who is used as a source for the details of the Battle of the Winwaed. *Historia Brittonum* tells us that Penda laid siege to Urbs Ludeu, the city where Oswiu resided. The precise location of this medieval city is unknown, but there are some indications it might be today's Stirling. Both Bede and *Historia Brittonum* agree that Oswiu tried to pay Penda for peace, but they disagree about what Penda did with the treasure. While *Historia Brittonum* claims Penda took the treasure and used it to reward his allies, Bede said he declined the payment, as his only goal was to completely eliminate all of Bernicia's people.

What Penda did next makes us wonder whether *Historia Brittonum* was right, as he turned his army south, probably toward home. However, there was a massive battle that happened somewhere in the region of Loidis (today's Leeds), and it could be because, according to Bede, Oswiu held Penda's son, Ecgfrith, as a hostage. Here, Penda was abandoned by his allies, most importantly Cadafael of Gwynedd, who deserted when Ethelwald of Deira did not want to join the battle and instead waited to see the outcome from a safe place. Perhaps Penda's allies deserted him, disappointed because he had declined the treasure offered by Oswiu at Urbs Ludeu. Or, if he did take the treasure, his allies were already paid and saw no reason to continue fighting.

Bede describes the flooding of the River Winwaed, which occurred after a series of heavy rains. To add to the hardship of dealing with the floodwaters, Penda's army was also attacked by Oswiu's forces. Most Mercians died during the battle, but as Bede tells it, more died by drowning in the river while trying to flee. Penda was killed, was along with King Ethelhere of East Anglia, and Oswiu became a dominant figure in Britain, although briefly. He allowed Penda's son Peada to rule the southern parts of Mercia, while he took the north for himself.

Even though Bede is regarded as the most reliable source for the history of this time, it is evident that he tried to obscure the importance of Penda since he was an enemy of Northumbria. However, modern history recognizes the significance of this Mercian king, who lifted his kingdom from the darkness in which his predecessors ruled to the heights of one of the most influential kingdoms of Anglo-Saxon Britain. The Battle of the Winwaed is also seen as the last battle between Christianity and paganism, as Penda's sons continued ruling as Christian kings. After the battle, Mercia was again divided, and its authority in the region was diminished. However, the Northumbrian lordship over Mercia ended within just a few years after this battle when Penda's son, Wulfhere, became the king.

Wulfhere (r. 658–675)

After the Battle of the Winwaed and Penda's death, Oswiu allowed Peada to rule the territories south of Mercia as a client state to Northumbria. However, Peada was murdered after only six months of ruling, supposedly by his own wife, Oswiu's daughter Alhflaed. Oswiu tried to install another subject king who would rule southern Mercia, but he eventually decided to rule all the lands by himself. The nobles of Mercia, Immin, Eafa, and Eadbeh, ignited a revolt as a result of this. They managed to lead the rebellion against Oswiu's rule and install their own king, Penda's second son Wulfhere. Oswiu couldn't allow himself to disperse his newly gained power in Britain by confronting the Mercians, so instead, he reached out to Wulfhere and recognized him as the new ruler of Mercia, installing his own kinsman as Mercian bishops. In return, Wulfhere continued to recognize Oswiu as his overlord. Despite that, Wulfhere managed to expand Mercian influence in the southern parts of Britain and forge a strong kingdom.

It is not known where Wulfhere was during the three years since the death of his father. Some historians believe he was in exile, while others trust Bede, who said it was the Mercian nobles who hid him and waited for their opportunity to install him as a king. Wulfhere was Mercia's first Christian king, and it was during his rule that

Mercia was converted to Christianity. However, there are no surviving documents that could tell us how Wulfhere became a Christian, as he certainly was not one while his father was still alive. Some scholars suggest he converted in order to please Oswiu and receive recognition as the king of Mercia. Others believe Wulfhere was influenced by his brother Peada, who had married Oswiu's Christian daughter and brought the first missionaries to Mercia to spread the religion. Nevertheless, it is this king we have to thank for the documents of Mercian origin, as the new monasteries and churches built during Wulfhere's rule started recording history as it unfolded. It is believed that the earliest document found in Mercia, the Tribal Hidage, dates from the time of Wulfhere.

Wulfhere married the Christian princess Eormenhild of Kent, and through that marriage, he brought Christianity even closer to Mercia since now the kinship and trade flowed through both kingdoms. The Christianization of Mercia continued uninterrupted, as the economic and political benefits it would bring were too great. Through kinship, Wulfhere tied Mercia with another Christian kingdom, Merovingian Gaul, which would give birth to the first kings of France. Wulfhere kept a close tie with the bishop of Northumbria, Wilfrid, to whom he gifted many acres of land. Wilfrid used that land to build churches and monasteries across Mercia. However, Wulfhere himself invested in a major monastery at Medeshamstede (today's Peterborough), and the 14th-century transcription of the document by which he endowed this monastery still survives. It is interesting that the document was signed by Wulfhere of Mercia, Oswiu of Northumbria, and Sigehere and Sebbi, the joint kings of Essex.

Wulfhere managed to achieve a lot for his kingdom through diplomatic and political resolutions. However, he was a successful war strategist as well. It was by means of warfare that he secured Mercian authority over the lands of the West Saxons, together with the Isle of Wight, in 661, where he brought Christianity. The Isle of

Wight and the territories of Meonware were granted to his godson, Ethelwealh (Æthelwealh) of the South Saxons, whose baptism Wulfhere sponsored during his efforts to spread Christian influence over satellite states such as Hwicce. He probably influenced his godson to marry the princess of Hwicce, Eafe, in order to support his efforts.

There is not much known about the relations between East Anglia and Mercia after the death of Ethelwold (Æthelwold) of East Anglia in 664. This kingdom was under the dominion of Northumbria before Wulfhere was crowned as the Mercian king. There is simply no mention of what happened to East Anglia after his succession. In Essex, Bede tells us that King Swithhelm was succeeded by the joint rulers Sigehere and Sebbi, who ruled under Wulfhere. However, it is unknown whether Wulfhere spread his authority in their territories with a sword or through diplomatic means. Bede also informs us that Sigehere and his people renounced Christianity and that it was Wulfhere who sent Bishop Jaruman of Lichfield to reconvert the East Saxons. This information still doesn't tell us what kind of relations existed between Essex and Mercia, but it does make it clear that Oswiu's influence in these territories was weaker and that Wulfhere was the dominant ruler there.

Wulfhere was recognized as the true king of Essex, but what is more important is that this lordship gave him access to the town of London. Being on the River Thames, London brought Mercia the ability to trade not just everywhere in Britain but also in Europe and Scandinavia. This privilege would stay with Mercia until the 9th century. Trade was an important source of wealth for the kings of the Early Middle Ages, and perhaps the possession of London was crucial in building Mercian supremacy over the Anglo-Saxon Heptarchy, a supremacy that would last up until the defeat of King Beornwulf of Mercia in 825.

However, it would turn out that Northumbria was to become the doom of King Wulfhere, just as it was for his father. Oswiu died of illness in 670 and was succeeded by his son Ecgfrith. It is possible that Wulfhere thought this change of power in Northumbria might weaken the kingdom, as he tried to attack it in 674, but Ecgfrith defeated the Mercians. Ecgfrith managed to do this despite the fact the Mercians came from a position of strength, as they had united all the southern tribes against Northumbria. Stephen of Ripon, in his *Life of St. Wilfrid*, a text from the 8th century, reports that Ecgfrith not only defeated Wulfhere but that he also forced him to surrender the lesser Kingdom of Lindsey and to pay tribute to Northumbria. However, Bede doesn't mention these events at all, nor does the *Anglo-Saxon Chronicle*. Wulfhere survived the battle against Ecgfrith, but he died a year later in 675, probably of disease, according to Henry of Huntington. He was succeeded by his brother Ethelred (Æthelred), who never achieved the supremacy of the south as Wulfhere did.

Ethelred (r. 675–704)

Ethelred was the third son of Penda, and he succeeded Wulfhere, probably because Wulfhere's son was too young to rule. This conclusion is drawn from the fact that Ethelred would abdicate the throne and leave it to Wulfhere's son Coenred instead of his own. However, we cannot be sure how Ethelred came to be king after his brother, as history is often obscure when it comes to such details in the Early Middle Ages, especially since there were no set rules of succession at the time. Ethelred ruled Mercia for the next thirty years as a Christian, and by all accounts, he was a very pious king. There is no information about his childhood and youth; he is practically not even mentioned in the sources until he became king.

His first act as king that is recorded in history was an attack on Kent in 676, where he destroyed Rochester, which was the seat of the West Kent bishops. There is no record of what could've been the reason for this attack, so scholars can only speculate using what little information they can from the political scene of that period. Some think the attack served as the defense of Surrey, a town that King

Hlothhere of Kent wished to conquer. Others believe Ethelred wanted to avenge his nephews, the sons of Eormenred of Kent. However, even the existence of Eormenred is questionable, as he only appears for the first time in hagiographies dated in later periods. Whatever the reason for the attack was, Ethelred managed to declare his dominion over Kent, and Hlothhere was forced to accept it.

Ethelred, just like his brother Peada, was married to a Northumbrian princess, who was also a daughter of Oswiu, named Osthryth. The year of their marriage is unknown, but it must have been somewhere before 679 since Bede mentions her as the Mercian queen before the Battle of the Trent, which took place in that year. Another thing that is unknown is the cause of this battle, but Bede gives us a description of its outcome. King Elfwine (Ælfwine) of Deira, who was the brother of both King Ecgfrith of Northumbria and Queen Osthryth of Mercia, died during the battle. He was loved in both kingdoms, and his death almost created animosity between Mercia and Northumbria. It was Theodore, the archbishop of Canterbury, who intervened to uphold the peace. After the battle, Ethelred took back the possession of Lindsey, which remained a part of the Kingdom of Mercia until the 9th century. It is believed that with the Battle of the Trent, Northumbrian interest in southern Britain effectively ended, though it was not the end of the conflicts with Mercia.

There is no evidence that Ethelred ever wanted to expand his kingdom to the south, like his brother Wulfhere did. Instead, he was content with influencing the dynastic power struggles in both Essex and Kent, and the charters by which Ethelred confirms the land grants of Kent to Kings Oswine and Swefheard survive to this day. Oswine ruled eastern Kent, while Swefheard, the son of Sebbi of Essex, ruled the western part. Perhaps it was the increasing power of Caedwalla and Ine, the kings of the West Saxons, that persuaded Ethelred not to pursue an invasion of the south. However, it is even more possible that Ethelred was preoccupied with wars against the

Welsh and could not afford to pursue his interests in the south, but almost nothing is known about the outcome of these wars.

The sign that the relations between Mercia and Northumbria weren't completely peaceful might be seen by the murder of Ethelred's wife, Osthryth, in 697. Bede wrote that she was killed by her own people, the Mercian nobles. Perhaps it was an act of revenge, as it was her sister Alhflaed who was accused of poisoning King Peada of Mercia. The real reason for her murder is unknown, but she was buried at Bardney, an abbey in Lindsey that both she and Ethelred founded and where she placed the bones of her uncle, Oswald of Northumbria, whose cult she started when he was proclaimed a saint.

In 704, Ethelred abdicated and became a monk, and later an abbot, in the same abbey where his wife was buried. It is peculiar that they chose to fund and support an abbey outside of the heart of Mercia, and historians see this as a sign of an effort to gain the patronage from provinces that lay on the edges of the kingdom. Ethelred continued to have some influence in the political life of Mercia, which Stephen of Ripon describes in his *Life of St. Wilfrid*. Ethelred advised his successor Coenred to make peace with Bishop Wilfrid, and his influence was also great enough to summon the king to his abbey.

It is unknown when Ethelred died, but both he and Queen Osthryth were venerated as saints at Bardney at a later date. This might have been a part of the policy of Ethelred's successors to start a cult of royal saints in the outlying territories in order to keep them loyal to Mercia. Ethelred, like his wife, was buried at Bardney Abbey.

Building the Kingdom

Since the reign of Penda, the geographical image of power in the Midland regions of Britain changed dramatically. It was he and his sons who started building Mercia, a kingdom that would keep dominating the political scene until the Viking invasions. The most critical point of Mercia's supremacy during the 8th and 9th centuries was their relationships with their neighbors. Through invasion, the Mercians incorporated around fifty regions, along with its tribes, under their rule. But it wasn't only warfare that brought territories and subjects under their control. It was through diplomacy, marriage, and trade with its neighbors that Mercia was able to build its authority.

It was Penda's sons who acknowledged that the kingdom was built mainly through diplomacy. They were the ones who realized that, in a battle for hegemony, it was important to convince the numerically superior British people that life would be better under Anglo-Saxon rule. Wulfhere and Ethelred offered security and protection to the Welsh Kingdoms of Gwynedd and Powys after a period of instability in the region that had been caused by Penda's death. Some kingdoms offered to become Mercian satellite states without resistance, such as Hwicce and the Magonsaete (Magonsæte), although some would argue that Hwicce was Penda's creation and was never a free kingdom.

Due to Wulfhere and his successors, Christianity spread across Mercia, bringing religious unity to people. It was this unity that offered sustainability and encouragement to the nation. Through religion, various tribes were united under the same God and into one nation. It was the Christian monks of Mercia who started recording history and creating sources for us to learn from, and as such, monasteries and churches did not serve only as places of worship. They served as archives for many documents that today give us an insight into the society of the Middle Ages. This is how we know that Mercians were predominantly warriors who were seeking an opportunity to prove themselves and build their prestige.

It is no wonder that a warrior society produced myths and legends of heroes to inspire whole generations into military service. One such inspired man became a legend himself. Guthlac, the son of Penwalh, a Mercian nobleman, gathered his own band of warriors from different tribes. Together, they indulged in various military adventures that set them apart from others and paved the path for their own immortality in stories. Guthlac served in the army of Ethelred, who was an extremely pious king. Probably inspired by the king's devotion to God, Guthlac became a monk when he was 24 years old. Even as an ascetic hermit, he continued to play a role in the political life of Mercia as he was the one who gave sanctuary to the future king Ethelbald (Æthelbald) when he was being pursued by his cousin Ceolred. It was men like Guthlac, warriors and saints, who in the company of kings and nobles built the Kingdom of Mercia. By standing ready for war or by recording events, documents, and various treaties, it was the people of Mercia who made the visions of kings come alive.

Chapter 3 – A New Dynasty

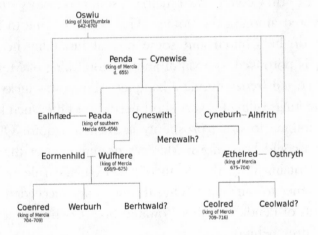

The family tree of King Coenred of Mercia

*https://upload.wikimedia.org/wikipedia/commons/thumb/0/0f/Aethelred_family_tr
ee.svg/800px-Aethelred_family_tree.svg.png*

Ethelred abdicated the throne and became a monk, leaving the
kingdom to his nephew, Coenred, who ruled from 704 until 709.
The new king seemed to have been as religious as his uncle because
he, too, abdicated and passed the throne of Mercia to his cousin,
Ethelred's son, Ceolred. Bede writes about Coenred with great
respect, and he recorded a story of the king's friend who was so
sinful that he was damned, even though Coenred pleaded for his

redemption. After only five years of rule, the Mercian king went to Rome, where Pope Constantine declared him a monk. Medieval chronicler William of Malmesbury cites Bede's story as a possible reason for Coenred's abdication; however, this is just speculation. It could also be that he was forced to abdicate by the Mercian nobles who favored his cousin, Ceolred. The practice of forcing kings to monasteries wasn't unusual in the Middle Ages. It was a way of peacefully transitioning power, as the former kings had to somehow be made unable to rule. Coenred stayed in Rome until the end of his days, and it wasn't recorded whether he ever had a wife or children.

Just as his predecessor, Ceolred did not achieve much as a king of Mercia, but part of that could be due to his short reign, which lasted from 709 to 716. Ceolred was Ethelred's son, and history suggests he wasn't favored amongst the nobles. This might be due to his poor treatment of the Church and some mental instability he suffered from. He is portrayed as a sinful and immoral king of Mercia who died in a crazed frenzy during a banquet. Mercia was lucky to have inadequate kings ruling for very short periods of time; such kings did close to nothing to bring prosperity to their kingdom. Otherwise, such rulers could bring down Mercia's dominion over the political scene of Britain. With the death of Ceolred, the rule of Penda's dynasty came to an end. The throne was succeeded by the descendants of Penda's brother Eowa, as both Coenred and Ceolred left no children behind.

The lack of signs of rivalry between the two lineages from the same royal family suggests they enjoyed mutual respect and cooperation and that it was only natural for the throne to be succeeded by Ethelbald, the grandson of Eowa. In fact, Mercian kings had a habit of appointing their own cousins and kinsmen in positions of power. This was a way to keep them close and loyal and to avoid dynastic power struggles in the kingdom.

What followed for Mercia was eighty years of stability and prosperity under two great kings, Ethelbald and Offa. Long reigns like these were very unusual for the Early Middle Ages, and the power of Mercia became even more pronounced by the political unrest in Northumbria, which had eleven kings during the rules of Ethelbald and Offa.

Ethelbald (r. 716-757)

The East Anglian monk Felix, in his manuscript *Life of Saint Guthlac*, tells us that Ethelbald was in exile during the reign of King Ceolred and that he befriended this saint who envisioned him as the next great king. Perhaps it was because of Ceolred's mistreatment of monasteries that Ethelbald sought allies among the clergy who would help him take the throne. The reason for Ethelbald's exile is unknown, but he returned to Mercia as soon as Ceolred died and began his reign. Almost nothing is known of his immediate family except that his father, Alweo, was Eowa's son.

Although the reigns of Coenred and Ceolred proved to not further Mercia, Ethelbald's reign brought renewed prosperity and political power to the kingdom. During the early years of his rule, he could do nothing more than to secure his position as a Mercian king and the founder of a new dynasty. The first opportunity to spread Mercian influence presented itself in 725 with the death of Wihtred of Kent, whose successors divided his kingdom into three parts. A year later, in 726, King Ine of Wessex abdicated and went on a pilgrimage to Rome. This kingdom was torn apart by power struggles due to multiple throne successors, and it is believed that Ethelbald helped Ethelheard (Æthelheard) become the new king of Wessex. Some even propose that the Mercian king was directly involved and that it was he who installed Ethelheard as the king. Whatever the case was, there are indicators that Wessex was now a subject to Mercian authority.

As for the situation in Kent, it is well known that Ethelbald was a patron of Kentish churches, but that is all that is mentioned about the Mercian king having any influence in Kent. No charter survives that would speak of his lordship over that kingdom. There are charters signed by Kentish Kings Ethelbert II and Eadberht I that do not mention the Mercian king as their overlord. Therefore, it is safe to assume Ethelbald missed the opportunity of King Wihtred's death to spread his influence over Kent.

Mercia had access to London through its control over Essex. But it was during the reign of Ethelbald that this town transferred to full Mercian control. As with Kent, there is no evidence in any charters that the Mercians had authority over Essex or the South Saxons, but we do have Bede's account from 731, who was a contemporary writer, that all these lands, together with all the provinces south of the Humber, were indeed subject to Ethelbald, the king of Mercia. It is possible that the charters with Ethelbald's name simply did not survive, but it is also possible that the practice of signing documents changed, and subject kings started signing only their own names.

Ethelbald had to organize military campaigns with the purpose of preserving his lordship, and the *Anglo-Saxon Chronicle* gives us an account of those wars. In 733, Ethelbald warred against Wessex and captured the royal manor of Somerton. About a decade later, in 740, Ethelheard of Wessex died and was succeeded by Cuthred, who attacked Ethelbald, probably in an attempt to free his kingdom from Mercian authority. However, he was unsuccessful. Three years later, Cuthred was allied with the Mercian king in the war against the Welsh. It could be that Ethelbald forced Cuthred, his subject, to serve during wartime as punishment for his earlier endeavors. The king of Wessex again tried to free his kingdom in 752 by opposing Ethelbald in another conflict. He possibly succeeded this time but only briefly, as there are records that confirm Ethelbald reasserted his authority over Wessex before the time of his death.

But it's not only Bede who claims Ethelbald was the king who ruled all the lands south of the Humber. There is another document that survives in its contemporary form, the Ismere Diploma. This is a charter dating from 736 in which Ethelbald of Mercia granted land to a certain Cyneberht to found a minster, a large or influential church.

This document starts by describing Ethelbald as the king of Mercia and all the provinces of South England. The Ismere Diploma also gives him the title of *Rex Britanniae*, "king of Britain." It is this title that speaks of Ethelbald's power more than anything else, as it can be seen as the Latin form of the Anglo-Saxon title *bretwalda*.

During the rule of Ethelbald, Mercia absorbed some of its satellite provinces and expanded the heartland of the kingdom. This practice would continue in the future under the rule of Offa. The rulers of these provinces, who were formerly independent kings, were now transformed into ealdormen. The title ealdorman was reserved for royal kin and those powerful nobles whose role in the kingdom was of such significance that they occupied the most prestigious offices. They were the ones who governed the provinces of the kingdom, commanded its armies, and dealt with local administration. Over time, the provinces were transformed into shires, and some of them are alive even today in the same form (for the most part).

Central to Ethelbald's reign was his relations with the Church. While in exile, he was friendly with Church magnates and the famous Guthlac, probably because he needed their influence to be appointed as king. Ethelbald was praised for giving alms to the poor, maintaining peace and justice throughout the kingdom, and defending the old and the widowed. However, he was strongly criticized for his personal life. In 746/47, an Anglo-Saxon missionary from Germany named Boniface and seven other bishops sent a letter to Ethelbald regarding his many sins. They accused him of indulging in his lustful thoughts and violating nuns, and they begged the king to stop with his sinful actions because he was not only condemning his own soul but also the soul of the whole nation, who looked up to him. They warned him that he was walking the path that would create a degenerate nation that would be weak in warfare and in faith. Boniface and the bishops advised the king to take a wife and abandon his life of sin. Ethelbald's failure to marry might have been the result of complex politics in the Mercian court, but there is no evidence to confirm such a belief.

There is more to Boniface's letter than the matters of the king's personal life. He accused Ethelbald of violating the Church's privileges, stealing from monasteries, and imposing forced labor on the clergy. In this part of the letter, the bishops accused the king, but they also expressed their worry about the reformation initiatives within the Frankish churches that could spread to the churches in England and influence the interests inside monasteries. The practice of granting land to the minsters without conditioning them to produce goods for the king was undermining the resources on which the kingdom could rely, and Ethelbald dealt with this problem by obliging all lands to provide labor, which Boniface saw as forced, oppressive, and violent. Pressured, Ethelbald offered an exemption to the churches, meaning they were no longer obliged to provide food, labor, or any other material tribute to the kingdom. However, he did retain the right to demand the clergy to provide him with services such as building bridges and defenses.

Ethelbald is not universally regarded as a good king. He was prone to giving in to violence, and he might have been involved in assassinations that would bring him political gain. The fact that he was murdered by a member of his own household in 757 only proves he was seen as an inadequate ruler. Bede's *Historia ecclesiastica gentis Anglorum* tells us that Ethelbald was murdered at Seckington, Warwickshire, by his own bodyguards and points out the possibility of treachery and betrayal. However, this part was added by an anonymous author after Bede's death, and there is no guarantee to its trustworthiness.

King Ethelbald was succeeded by Beornred, who was probably a member of a rival dynasty. This suggests the possibility of a coup d'état, but there is no strong evidence to support this claim. Ethelbald was buried at Repton, where a fragment of a cross was found that depicts a man with a crown on his head, wielding a sword and a shield, and mounted on a horse. If this is proven to be a representation of Ethelbald, it would be the earliest image of an English king.

Beornred ruled for only one year before he was defeated and succeeded by Offa. His rule was marked by a lack of support, and the *Peterborough Chronicle*, which is a part of the *Anglo-Saxon Chronicle*, mentions it as an unhappy year.

Offa, however, presented himself as a much more suitable successor as he was Ethelbald's twice-removed cousin who could trace his lineage to Pybba and Eowa.

Offa (r. 757–796)

Offa was not just one of the most important Mercian rulers; he was also one of the most important leaders of all of Britain. However, there is no surviving contemporary biography of this king. Thus, the *Anglo-Saxon Chronicle* serves as the main source of information about his times. Since the document originated in Wessex, the *Anglo-Saxon Chronicle* might be very biased and may not show the real extent of Mercian power in Britain. Fortunately, some Mercian charters from Offa's times do exist, and they speak of a more accurate political stage and authority during Offa's reign. Unfortunately, Bede's *Historia ecclesiastica gentis Anglorum* ends with the events of 731 and does not record anything about Offa, but it does provide the background for his reign.

Offa did not inherit the throne from his predecessor. The fact that he had to fight for it tells us Mercia was in the midst of a dynastic struggle. It is quite possible that Offa had to reestablish Mercian authority over some satellite states after the succession conflict. But he was quick and powerful enough to do so, as the documents from the beginning of his reign show that the Hwiccan king was under Offa's authority. The royal dynasty of the Kingdom of Lindsey ceased to exist during the early years of Offa's reign, so it is possible he managed to take control of its territories entirely. However, Mercian control over the lands of southern England collapsed after the death of Ethelbald. It would take some time until Offa would succeed in reestablishing that lordship, as Mercia was often in conflict with the Welsh kingdoms from the start of Offa's reign.

In 760, there was a battle between the Mercians and Welsh at Hereford. There had been decades of hostility between King Ethelbald and the Welsh Kingdoms of Brycheiniog, Gwent, and Powys. This hostility culminated when Offa took the Mercian throne. The outcome was not good for Mercia, as the Welsh kingdoms finally regained their independence from Anglo-Saxon influence. Offa would continue to try and reestablish his authority in the Welsh territories, though, as there are records of repeated conflicts in 778, 784, and 796.

It is believed that during one of these conflicts, Offa ordered the construction of a dike. This dike still exists, and it roughly follows the modern border between Wales and England. The dike was named after Offa by scholars, but it is unknown if he was the one who actually built it. The purpose of the dike is still being debated, as well as the year of construction. Modern radiocarbon dating is challenging the opinion that it was built during the Early Middle Ages and places the start of the construction in the early 5th century. The construction of the dike might have started earlier, but the earthwork was continued in Offa's time. The way it was built, with the displaced soil on the Mercian side and a ditch on the Welsh, suggests the dike was built by the Mercians as a defensive earthwork.

There is a source from the 9th century that confirms the opinion of historians that the dike was built by Offa. Asser, a Welsh monk, wrote that not long before his time, there was a king named Offa, and all the surrounding kingdoms were terrified of him. He continues, saying that Offa built a great dike between Wales and Mercia, from sea to sea. The ability to raise both the resources and labor for such a great construction work tells us more about Offa's authority than any other document that survived. Although history often overlooks Offa because of a lack of written evidence, he must have been a truly great king, perhaps even the greatest Mercian ruler. The dike is 240 kilometers long (150 miles), and it does follow the Welsh-English border from sea to sea. It was probably never a border on which both kingdoms agreed, and it is not a continuous line, as it is often interrupted in places where natural barriers exist. The dike is still being examined and is still a subject of much speculation.

Sometime after 762, when King Ethelbert II of Kent died, Offa started signing charters in which he granted the land of Kent to various individuals or church institutions, with the names of Kentish kings as witnesses. This means that he managed to impose his authority over this kingdom eventually. Kent did have a tradition of joint rulers, where one would rule the east and the other one the west. As one or the other had to act as a supreme king, conflicts were normal. Offa probably took advantage of one such conflict to subdue Kent and put it under Mercian rule. It is unclear for how long Kent acted as a subject to the Kingdom of Mercia, but scholars believe that some resistance to Offa's rule must have existed. For instance, there was the Battle of Otford in 776 between Kent and Mercia, but its outcome is unknown. Because there is no evidence of Offa signing the charters anymore, it is generally believed that Kent managed to gain its independence, and since the charter from 784 was signed by King Ealhmund of Kent alone, we can conclude that Mercia was indeed defeated at the Battle of Otford.

Offa reappears in the Kentish charters from 785/86, and his renewed authority is clear. However, he did not just act as the overlord of Kent but as its sole ruler as well. Kent was reduced to a Mercian province, and its royal dynasty was eliminated. Mercia kept full control of Kent until Offa's death in 796.

Same as in Kent, Offa was involved in the affairs of the Kingdom of Sussex, and the evidence for this is found in the charters. However, the course of events, such as when and how Sussex fell under Mercian rule, is not clear. Several kings ruled Sussex at the same time, and this implies Sussex was not a single kingdom. Local kings probably recognized Offa's authority early during his reign, but evidence of some resistance exists. Records of Offa defeating the people of Hastings in 771 originates from the 12th century from the chronicler Symeon of Durham. This might just be a record of Offa's extension of authority over the whole Kingdom of Sussex, while some of its parts recognized him as an overlord at a much earlier date. After 772, there is no evidence of Mercian authority over Sussex until 790, which implies that either the charters that mention him are to be doubted or that Sussex gained independence to some extent, however briefly.

When it comes to East Anglia, there is evidence that it was independent during the early years of Offa's reign, as King Beonna (r. 749-760 or 758-760) issued his own coins. He was also the first British king who included his title and not just his name on the coins. King Ethelberht (Æthelberht) II of East Anglia (r.?-794) was also independent long enough to issue his own coins. However, the *Anglo-Saxon Chronicle* records Offa ordering the death of King Ethelberht. This and the fact that Offa issued coins in East Anglia from the early 790s implies his authority. It is possible that Ethelberht rose up in a rebellion against Offa, who then ordered his death as a punishment. There is a possibility that Offa's wife, Cynethryth, was involved in the murder of the East Anglian king, but historians regard these stories as legends since they were first mentioned during the late 11th century.

In 757, Cynewulf became the king of Wessex, and he was successful in regaining the territories of his kingdom, which were previously taken by King Ethelbald of Mercia. At the Battle of Bensington in 779, Offa won against Cynewulf and took the lands around the Thames for Mercia. It is commonly believed that it was at this time that Wessex recognized the overlordship of the Mercian king, even though there is no evidence to support this claim. Cynewulf was murdered in 786 in a dynastic dispute, and he was succeeded by Beorhtric, whose placement on the throne of Wessex was probably with Offa's support. Beorhtric recognized Offa's authority from the beginning of his rule, and he used the Mercian currency throughout his kingdom, issuing his own coins only after Offa died. Beorhtric also married Offa's daughter, Eadburg, in 789, and the two kings joined forces to exile Ecgberht, the son of Ealhmund of Kent, to Francia. Asser, a biographer from the 9th century, wrote about Queen Eadburg, who gained power over the whole Kingdom of Wessex and who behaved as tyrannically as her father. It is possible that she was allowed to exercise her power out of fear toward her father, Offa.

As for Northumbria, there is no evidence that it was under Mercian rule at any time of Offa's reign. However, the relations between the two kingdoms were probably good and steady since Offa's second daughter, Elfflaed (Ælfflæd), married Ethelred I of Northumbria in 792.

Offa and the Church

Offa's intervention in the matters of Kent in the 760s placed him in conflict with Archbishop of Canterbury Jaenberht (Jænberht), who gave his support to Ecgberht II of Kent. Offa revoked all the contributions to Canterbury made by Ecgberht, while Jaenberht claimed the monastery of Cookham, which was clearly on Offa's land and, therefore, his possession.

The first papal mission into British Christian territory happened during Offa's rule. The only mission before that was the one when Pope Gregory the Great sent Augustine to start the Christianization of the Anglo-Saxons in 597. In 786, Pope Adrian I sent his legates to evaluate the state and church and to bring various ecclesiastical decrees to help guide the kings, nobles, clergy, and people. The legates were George and Theophylact, the bishops of Ostia and Todi, respectively. They were first received at Canterbury and then at Offa's court, where a council was held to discuss the goals of the mission. The king of the West Saxons, Cynewulf, was also present at this council.

At the council, it was decided that George would go to Northumbria, while Theophylact would stay in Mercia, and from there, he would visit other parts of Britain. A report of the mission written by George, which was sent to Pope Adrian, survived. It contains all the details about the events that took place at the Northumbrian council. But we have no such report from Theophylact's mission. After his mission in Northumbria was concluded, George returned to Mercia, where another council was held at Offa's court. This time it was in the presence of Jaenberht, the archbishop of Canterbury, and the council issued more canons that described the rights and daily life of the English people.

Only a year later, in 787, Offa established an archdiocese at Lichfield, thus reducing the power of Canterbury. It is not clear if he did this on purpose because he was in conflict with Jaenberht, but it is believed that the issue was discussed with the papal legates just a year earlier. The first archbishop of Lichfield was Hygeberht, who received a pallium, a symbol of his new authority, directly from Rome. This is why historians believe that the papal legates approved of the new archdiocese. Canterbury remained an archdiocese for the south and southeast, while Lichfield included Worcester, Hereford, Leicester, Lindsey, and some parts of the Midlands.

The accounts of these events that survived through history come from King Coenwulf of Mercia and Pope Leo III from 798. While Coenwulf states that the new archdiocese at Lichfield was created just to spite the archbishop of Canterbury, the pope wrote that the only reason for its creation was the size of the Kingdom of Mercia. However, both Coenwulf and Leo had their own reasons to stand firm when it came to this subject. Coenwulf wanted London to become the archdiocese of the whole south, while the pope did not want to allow Rome's decisions to be questioned. There is another source that seems to confirm the belief that Offa created an archdiocese at Lichfield in order to gain even more control and power. A letter from the Yorkish scholar Alcuin to Archbishop

Ethelhard (Æthelhard) of Canterbury gives his opinion that the motive was not a reasonable consideration but more a desire for power.

There might be another reason for the creation of the archdiocese at Lichfield, however, and it concerns Offa's son, Ecgfrith. As soon as Hygeberht was elevated to the position of archbishop, he performed the ritual of consecration for Ecgfrith, elevating his royal status to king. This is the first such ceremony performed in England, and it is possible that Jaenberht of Canterbury refused to perform the consecration before. It was unusual in England of that period to proclaim a king while the actual king was still alive and occupying the throne. It is possible that Offa heard of Pope Adrian I consecrating the sons of Charlemagne, Pippin (or Pepin), and Louis, as kings, and he wanted the same prestige for his own son, but the Anglo-Saxon tradition wouldn't allow it. However, Offa continued to respect the office of Canterbury, as Jaenberht was regarded as a senior cleric in all matters to Hygeberht. After Jaenberht died in 792, the archbishop of Lichfield became the senior cleric. The new archbishop of Canterbury, Ethelhard, was able to sign decrees, witness charters, and preside at synods without Hygeberht. This means that Canterbury's authority still had Offa's respect.

In one letter to Charlemagne, Pope Adrian describes rumors he heard about Offa proposing to Charlemagne to conspire against him and install a Frankish pope in Rome. However, Adrian continued by saying he was certain that the rumors were started by Offa's political enemies, although he did not name them. The precise date of this letter is unknown, and it could be from anywhere between 784 and 791. It might be that this letter was related to the papal legate's mission in Britain from 786, as George and Theophylact would have been perfect as the bearers of the rumor, but we cannot know with certainty.

Offa founded many churches and monasteries, most of them devoted to Saint Peter. He was praised by Alcuin of York, who was

Charlemagne's advisor, for his generosity and piety. Offa also worked hard in instructing his subjects in the ways of the Church and Christianity. He even promised a yearly present to Rome of 365 mancuses (a measure of either a golden coin or thirty silver pence). Offa was aware that the Church would take care of his family once he was gone, so he acquired papal privileges and ensured the monasteries and abbeys he founded remained in his wife's and children's possession after his death.

Offa's Politics

There are documents and letters from which we can draw conclusions on Offa's diplomatic relations with Europe, but they are all from the last ten years of his reign. Alcuin of York wrote to Offa several times, and his letters that date from the 780s onward are preserved. In them, he greets Offa's wife and children, and he congratulates the king on his efforts to encourage education in Mercia. Charlemagne sent a proposal to Offa in which he wished his son Charles to marry one of the Mercian princesses, probably Elfflaed, Offa's daughter. The Mercian king replied that his son Ecgfrith should marry Charlemagne's daughter Bertha. For some reason, Charlemagne found this offensive, and he decided to break contact with England. In addition, he banned all English ships from entering French harbors. The letters from Alcuin, who was Charlemagne's advisor, make it very clear that this situation wasn't resolved until the 790s. In 794, Charlemagne sought help from the English Church at the council of Frankfurt, in which many political and religious issues were raised.

In 796, Charlemagne wrote a letter to Offa concerning the status of English pilgrims on the continent. This letter is the first surviving document of English diplomacy in history, but it also reveals what kind of relationship the two kings had with each other. Charlemagne refers to Offa as his "brother." He also mentions trade between the two kingdoms in black stone and cloaks (or cloths). It is interesting that Charlemagne took in exiles from England who were openly

Offa's enemies, such as Eadberht III Praen (Præn), who later became the king of Kent, or Ecgberht of Wessex. This proves that diplomacy between the Anglo-Saxon kingdoms and the Franks was fairly complicated. Clearly, Offa was a minor figure when compared to Charlemagne, who ruled an empire that stretched from the Atlantic Ocean to the Pannonian Plain. However, they were close enough to name each other "brother." On the other hand, there was a constant struggle between the two rulers, which is depicted through their open support for each other's enemies.

When it comes to the internal politics of Offa's Mercia, we do not have many surviving sources. There are some charters that refer to Offa as *Rex Merciorum* ("King of the Mercians"), but on some occasions, he was mentioned as "King of Mercians and surrounding nations." There are some charters that refer to him as *Rex Anglorum* ("King of England"), but there is a strong belief that these were forged documents that appeared later, probably dating from the 10th century when this title was used by all kings. The best evidence of Offa's status in England is from the coins he issued. Some of them contain the markings "Of R A," which can mean "Rex Anglorum," but this remains to be proven. If it does stand for "King of England," it would be as a statement of his power rather than as the ruler of all of England.

Offa constructed some of the fortified towns, or burhs/burgs, and it is believed that they included Bedford, Hereford, Northampton, Oxford, and Stamford. These towns provided defenses during wartime, but they also served as administrative centers of the kingdom and as regional markets. It was these markets that brought economic change to England, but there is a belief that Offa himself did not recognize the change during his reign. The economy simply shifted its center point from the farms to these fortified towns, a fact which later kings would be able to exploit. Offa also issued laws in his own name, but no details about them survived. We know about them only because Alfred the Great (r. 847–899) mentioned them in the introduction to his own code of law. Alfred's code includes some of the laws of Offa, Ine of Wessex, and Ethelbert of Kent; however, it is not specified which laws are taken from which king. Alfred only mentions he used the laws that seemed just to him.

Offa died on July 29th, 796, and was succeeded by his son Ecgfrith, who only ruled for 141 days, at least according to the *Anglo-Saxon Chronicle*. There is evidence that supports Alcuin's claim that Offa went to great lengths to secure his son's succession. It is possible Offa killed all of the dynastic rivals of his son, as many contemporary writers mention all the blood he spilled in his son's name. The fact that Ecgfrith was succeeded by Coenwulf, who was only distantly related to Offa, may support this claim.

Coenwulf (r. 796-821) and Dynastic Rivalry

King Coenwulf of Mercia was a descendant of Penda's sibling Coenwealh. Through this descendancy, Coenwulf was related to Offa and his son Ecgfrith. Offa must have kept him in high regard as there is evidence that Coenwulf witnessed charters during his rule. Coenwulf also had connections to the royal dynasty of Hwicce through this kinship, which suggests his family was powerful although not directly connected to the Mercian royal lineage. A year after Coenwulf succeeded the throne, Alcuin wrote a letter to the people of Kent, lamenting that there was hardly anyone left of the old royal stock. He may have been referring to Coenwulf, but it is not clear, as Eardwulf of Northumbria took the throne in 796 as well. It is possible Alcuin was referring to both new kings when he made his remark. However, we do know Alcuin had a negative opinion of Coenwulf. He saw him as a tyrant, and he often criticized his decision to leave his wife in favor of another. This might be reason enough for Alcuin to belittle the new Mercian king.

Coenwulf's early rule was marked by a loss of control over the southern English territories. There is evidence that Mercia lost control of East Anglia, as they started stamping their own coinage. Also, Wessex became estranged by the time of Coenwulf's rule, and

Kent started an uprising. There are implications that suggest that this uprising started in the last years of Offa's rule, but it was during Coenwulf's reign that Kent gained Carolingian support, as their future king, Eadberht III Praen, was living in exile at Charlemagne's court. When Eadberht became the king, Ethelhard, the archbishop of Canterbury, fled his diocese, probably because it was ransacked.

This situation in Kent might have been avoided if Coenwulf wouldn't have hesitated to act. However, he did not want to do so without the pope's approval. The reason for his hesitation might have lain in the fact that Eadberht, while in exile, became a priest, and Coenwulf did not want to be responsible for the murder of a clergyman. This was why he sent a letter to Pope Leo III, explaining that, as a priest, Eadberht renounced any right to the throne. However, he did ask the pope to move the seat of the southern archbishopric from Canterbury to London, probably since he already lost control over Kent. Leo III refused to move the seat, but in the same letter, he called for the action of removing Eadberht from the throne as well as excommunicating him. He even made a threat of applying those punishments to every prince of England. Furthermore, the people of England were told to expel the new king of Kent in order to save his soul.

Upon receiving the pope's letter in 798, Coenwulf finally acted and attacked Kent. After a short struggle, the Mercians captured Eadberht, gouged his eyes out, and cut off his hands. Coenwulf imprisoned the king of Kent at Winchcombe, a religious house of Mercia, and Coenwulf offered the rule of Kent to his brother Cuthred, who ruled it from 801 until his death in 807. It was during his rule that the archbishopric of Lichfield was abolished on October 12th, 803. Once this happened, Canterbury regained the status of archbishopric of the Midlands and southern regions. Cuthred did live to see the first Viking raids on the shores of Britain, but after his death, Coenwulf started ruling Kent. In the charter from 809, he is titled "King of the Mercians and the Province of Kent."

The Kingdom of Essex remained under Mercian control during Coenwulf's reign, just as it did during Offa's. The throne of Essex passed from Sigeric I, who left for Rome in 798 and abdicated, to his son Sigered. Sigered appears on several charters issued by Coenwulf, and he even witnessed one of the charters as king in 811, but in later charters, he is referred to as a sub-king and afterward as a *dux* or ealdorman. This means that Coenwulf integrated Essex into his kingdom, completely depriving its king of any power, though the ealdorman did rule with some degree of autonomy.

Northumbria invaded Mercia in 801, probably because Coenwulf gave refuge to the enemies of the new Northumbrian king, Eardwulf. However, there is no record of the battles and their outcome, but peace was concluded on equal terms.

There is no clear evidence of what happened with East Anglia, but by 805, Coenwulf started issuing his coins there, which leads one to the conclusion that if East Anglia gained independence, it lasted for only a short time before Coenwulf managed to set his authority over it once more. The relations with Wessex were more complicated, as its new king, Ecgberht, was also in exile at the court of Charlemagne. Ecgberht ruled independently of Mercia since the beginning of his reign in 802, and Coenwulf never managed to reestablish Mercian authority over Wessex. However, Coenwulf was the only Anglo-Saxon king who gained the title "emperor" prior to the 10th century.

During Coenwulf's reign, Mercia warred against the Welsh kingdoms, possibly in 796 or 797. The first battle took place at Rhuddlan, which was located in Mercia territory, but in 798, Coenwulf took the opportunity to invade. In this campaign, he killed Caradog Ap Meirion, the king of Gwynedd. Another opportunity to attack the Welsh was found after the civil war in Gwynedd in 816 when Hywel ap Caradog took the throne. This time, the Mercians took control over the Welsh territories of Snowdonia and Rhufuniog, and in 819, Coenwulf raided Dyfed. There was a battle at

Lhanvaes (on the Isle of Anglesey) in 817/18, but there is no mention of Mercians in the surviving records of the battle.

In Coenwulf's charters that were issued between 804 and 817, Elfthryth (Ælfthryth) is mentioned as his wife. His daughter was Cwenthryth, and she inherited Winchcombe Abbey as it was the patrimony of their family. She was engaged in a dispute about this inheritance with Archbishop of Canterbury Wulfred, and this is how she is known to history. There is also a record of Coenwulf's son, Cynehelm, who later became a saint. Ealhswith, the wife of Albert the Great, is said to have been the descendant of Coenwulf through her mother's side of the family; however, Asser, the biographer, didn't leave any further details.

In 821, Coenwulf died at Basingwerk in Flintshire. It is believed that he died while preparing a campaign against the Welsh, but the cause of his death remains unknown. He was succeeded by his brother Ceolwulf I, who had to deal with a dynastic dispute at the beginning of his reign. Coenwulf was the last of the great Mercian kings. After his reign, Mercia lost supremacy and started to decay.

After the death of Coenwulf, Mercia entered its period of decline, and the dynastic troubles were felt early on. Coenwulf's son, Cynehelm, fell victim to the rivalry between the noble houses, and he was killed in 811. His cult was established by his family, with the seat of it located at Winchcombe. It was this cult that brought prestige and riches to the family, who continued to fight for control over Mercia. Ceolwulf, Coenwulf's brother, took the throne, but he wasn't strong enough as a king to keep the stability he inherited. Coenwulf's consecration was even delayed for a year because after his death, many disagreements and arguments arose between the nobles, bishops, and other kings who wanted to divide Mercia or gain some authority over its shires.

Ceolwulf ruled until 823 when he was deposed by Beornwulf, who was stronger and who managed to exploit the situation in Mercia to his own gain. Beornwulf is mentioned in two charters, one from

812 by King Coenwulf and another one from 823 by King Ceolwulf. In both charters, he is mentioned as a low-ranking noble. It is interesting that a low-ranking nobleman managed to rise and become a king. It is unknown whether he was connected to the royal family, but the surviving evidence suggests he wasn't. The royal family always took up high positions, and Alcuin already informed us that there was hardly anyone left of royal stock. Beornwulf's rule wasn't long either; he only ruled from 823 to 826, and it was during his reign that Mercia lost any supremacy over other kingdoms of the Anglo-Saxon Heptarchy.

Mercian military power declined together with its supremacy. Beornwulf tried to attack the West Saxons, for reasons unknown, but he lost. The battle took place at Ellandun (today's Wroughton), and the defeat of Beornwulf's army is seen by historians as the true beginning of Mercia's decline. The pro-Mercian king of Kent, Baldred, was defeated by Ethelwulf (Æthelwulf), the son of Ecgberht of Wessex in 826. By driving out Baldred, Wessex took control over Kent.

Mercia's grasp over southern England was at its end. Essex and Sussex both chose to offer their loyalty to Wessex instead. East Anglia rebelled against Mercia, and they asked Ecgberht for help. While trying to put down the rebellion, Beornwulf was killed in East Anglia in 826. Beornwulf was succeeded by one of his ealdormen, Ludeca, who only ruled for one year. The East Anglian rebellion continued, and in yet another attempt to put an end to it, Ludeca was killed in 827.

Another short-lived king then rose to power in Mercia. Wiglaf, whose ancestry is uncertain, rose to power immediately after Ludeca's death. He ruled until 829, which was when he lost the kingdom to Ecgberht of Wessex. However, Ecgberht only ruled for one year over Mercia, as Wiglaf managed to take the throne back and rule for another nine years, dying in 839.

It is believed that Wiglaf was connected to the powerful 7th-century King Penda of Mercia. One of the records that survived the passage of time mentions Wigstan as a descendant of Coenred, Penda's grandson. Because only Wigstan's name is recorded, we cannot be sure if he was Penda's descendant through his mother's line or through his father's. This means that there is a possibility Wiglaf was also Penda's descendant, but there is no firm evidence to support this presumption.

As mentioned above, Mercia was invaded by Wessex after only two years of Wiglaf's rule. Ecgberht was successful in his campaign against Mercia, and he drove Wiglaf away, but he did not kill him. Wessex now had complete superiority over the southern regions of England, and soon, Northumbria submitted as well.

Ecgberht became known as the eighth *bretwalda* in the *Anglo-Saxon Chronicle*, the eighth ruler of Britain. Ecgberht kept Mercia under his control for one year, but it was enough to issue his own coins, which depict him with the title of *Rex Merciorum*—"King of Mercia." In 830, Wiglaf managed to retake Mercia, probably by force. If Ecgberht gave the kingdom back to Wiglaf, it would've been recorded as an event in the *Anglo-Saxon Chronicle*. The way it is written leaves enough room for speculation, though. Because Wiglaf started issuing charters once more, we have evidence that Mercia was a completely independent kingdom again. This means that Wiglaf did not rule as a sub-king to Ecgberht. Because he mentions bishops, magistrates, and ealdormen in these charters, it is safe to presume that Wiglaf did not regain only Mercia but also some authority over the Church in the southern territories.

A charter from 836 records a council in Leicestershire, and among the attendees were the archbishop of Canterbury and eleven bishops. Another charter, dating from between 829 and 837, shows that King Sigeric II of Essex signed as a witness, which may indicate Essex was once more under the dominion of Mercia. London remained in Mercian hands throughout the second half of King

Wiglaf's reign, and it is surprising that Wessex was willing to lose such a strategically important town. This is another piece of evidence that supports the presumption that Mercia gained independence through force. Among the territories that were recovered by the Mercians was Wales, but it is not recorded whether this was done by Wiglaf or by his successor, Beorhtwulf.

It seemed like Mercia was recovering after its sudden decline, but the Mercian kings never managed to regain their authority over other southeastern kingdoms. East Anglia gained its independence and started issuing its own coins, which implies that after they drove back Wessex, they did not fall under Mercian rule. Wessex did rise to power suddenly during the late 820s, but it did not manage to keep its authority over other kingdoms. Historians tend to think that it was Mercia's dynastic troubles that gave the opportunity for Wessex to rise, and once Wiglaf proved to be a strong king, Ecgberht wasn't able to retain the dominant position of Wessex. There are other theories of why Wessex failed to maintain their dominion, but the lack of evidence and records makes it hard to evaluate them.

Mercia would never fully recover after the losses of the southern territories, though. Essex was probably the only kingdom that returned under Mercian control, but we cannot be sure whether this was by force or by the will of King Sigeric II of Essex, who might have sought an ally in Wiglaf. It is not precisely known when Wiglaf died, but by tracing the rule of the next few kings in the *Anglo-Saxon Chronicle*, we can see that Burgred reigned for 22 years before he was driven out of Mercia by the Vikings. This means his rule started in 852. His predecessor was Beorhtwulf, who ruled for thirteen years, which means he succeeded the throne in 839, which is probably the year of Wiglaf's death. There is a possibility Wiglaf was succeeded by his son Wigmund instead of Beorhtwulf. However, he is mentioned as a king in only one record, which is of debatable origin anyway, and so, this information should be regarded with suspicion.

The dynastic troubles in Mercia continued after Wiglaf's death, and this unrest proved to be fatal for Mercia. In contrast, Ecgberht of Wessex established a strong dynasty that continued to spread its influence throughout southern England.

Upon the death of Wiglaf, his heir and grandson, Wigstan, refused the throne in order to become a monk. This is how Beorhtwulf became a king. There is a possibility he was Wigstan's great-uncle, as William of Malmesbury, a historian from the 12th century, notes this. According to him, Beorfrith, the son of Beorhtwulf, wished to marry Wigstan's mother, Queen Elfflaed (Wiglaf's widow), but Wigstan refused the offer since they were too closely related. According to William, Beorfrith was so angry that he struck Wigstan with his dagger, killing him. In the story of William of Malmesbury, Wigstan is a young king. Since there are no other records of him being a king, it is safe to presume that the story is not true. Wigstan did become a saint after his death, though, and his cult is one of martyrdom.

Chapter 4 – Court, Church, Country, and the People

Christianity played a significant role in the lives of medieval commoners, kings, and queens alike. The Church had its expectations of how a king should govern his kingdom, but the people were free enough to express their thoughts. As the spiritual leaders of the people, it was expected that the Church would guide the kings in their rule and help them fulfill their obligations. While the archbishops, bishops, and clerics were the religious leaders of the country, the kings were its secular leaders. But the boundary between the two was never clear enough, as it was believed that the king was appointed by God himself. As such, kings often thought themselves to be above the law of humans, and they displayed tyrannical behaviors, while, at the same time, they were afraid for their souls and were extraordinarily pious. This conflict between religion and state existed throughout the centuries, as we have evidence of a constant struggle between the Church and the kings. The land was gifted, then taken away, and so were the blessings and the protections that the Church could offer.

This duality in the lives of kings can best be portrayed through the letter of Boniface and his bishops to King Ethelbald of Mercia. The king is praised for his generosity, for aiding the widows and poor, almsgiving, and punishing criminals, such as thieves. The king had ecclesiastical approval for his deeds, and he was generally seen as a good king to his people. But his personal life was completely the opposite, and Boniface begged him to change. The king was unmarried and accused of sinful lust, which he would drown by abusing nuns and virgins who were devoted to God. Ethelbald also pressed hard against the Church, often taking away their revenues and privileges.

Perhaps the conflict between the Church and the kings was affected by the tradition of Germanic kingship, which had been preserved since the Anglo-Saxon invasion and which had survived well into the Kingdom of England. The Germanic tradition of kingship referred to the fact that leaders were there to maintain order and provide justice and protection for the people. While this was all well within the Christian doctrine, it wasn't enough for the Church. The Christian king was expected to set a good example of modesty and a spiritual way of life for his people. He should model his life as if he was a part of the ecclesiastical order. But the kings were often greedy, violent, and cruel. As Alcuin advised Coenwulf, the Church expected the kings to lead by example, to promote faith among their people, and to protect and honor the Church. As the king was above all others, so should he be above others with his sense of morality, duty, and love of God.

Kings rarely openly defied the Church since it was the Church that gave them a voice and power through their recognition as the servants appointed by God. They avoided the accusations of the Church regarding their private lives and personal immorality, and in doing so, they rewarded the Church with land or new shrines to various saints. In return, the Church turned a blind eye to a king's personal misbehaviors. However, the Church would do it as long as it suited them. Both Offa and Ethelbald were generous in giving money and land to the Church. Offa is famous for his personal connection to Saint Peter, to whom he devoted many shrines. He founded and gifted many minsters and abbeys with both land and riches. Ethelbald was famous for his alms and for building a shrine for Saint Guthlac, a shrine richly decorated with golden ornaments. He also founded the Crowland Abbey. Yet both of these Mercian kings are remembered as "despoilers" of the Church, as they both took advantage of the privileges offered by the Church. Both Ethelbald and Offa had expectations for the Church to provide for them. They regarded the land of the Church as their families' personal ventures that should bring them income.

The Church integrated itself in the kingdom, and by doing so, it allowed the secular rulers to take part in the affairs of the Church. During the second half of the 8th century, kings participated in the religious councils known as synods. This was needed because, at these councils, the bishops were free to negotiate certain religious privileges and immunities that only the kings could grant. The manuscripts and notes left behind by the church councils inform us that in 747, Ethelbald was part of the synod at Closfesho (unknown location), where he listened to the problems of drunkenness in monasteries and the rising of immorality. At a similar council two years later, Ethelbald was forced to agree on specific compromises regarding church land and the obligations of clerics.

The lives of the kings were intertwined with the lives of the archbishops and bishops, and the medieval Anglo-Saxon kingdoms wouldn't have existed without the support of the Church. Many kings became religious figures in the form of saints, a practice that would not just immortalize a king but would also introduce a cult of his persona. This cult would draw pilgrims and people from all around the kingdom to a dedicated shrine, and the shrines would eventually develop into monasteries or churches, which attracted even more people. Many villages and towns developed around monasteries, and it was these territories that were the possessions of kings and queens. A royal family had its prestige by having an ancestor who was a saint, and with that prestige came the possession of lands around the shrine of their sanctified ancestor. This was land that took care of the people who either cultivated it or who were craftsmen and merchants. No matter what the people did, they were the ones who brought riches to the kings and queens through various taxes.

The Mercian Court

Unfortunately, the first record about life at Anglo-Saxon courts dates from the reign of King Alfred the Great of Wessex, who ruled in the 9th century. No record of Mercian court life survived, but historians have tried to reconstruct it. Alfred wrote extensively on the needs of the kings and his court. He said that in order to do his work that was appointed by God, he needed certain tools and materials. He noted that the tools were priests, soldiers, and workers, while the materials were the land and various gifts, such as food, clothes, and ale, with which he could sustain the priests, the soldiers, and the workers. Without any of these, a king wouldn't be able to perform the task he was appointed to. He wouldn't be able to develop the kingdom and protect its people.

The Mercian kings must have had similar needs for their kingdoms. In the late 8th century, Alcuin gave advice to Coenwulf about another great need of a king—the wise counselors who feared God, loved justice, and sought peace with their friends. Kingship was a very personal matter, but it could not function properly if the king was alone. He needed the support and the advice of his most trusted men in both matters of the court and matters of the country. Naturally, kings sought their own family members as advisors, but they also looked outside it. The king needed talented people, and if they couldn't be found in the family, he would have to search elsewhere. This is how courts became gathering places for people with various skills, abilities, and social standings, whether they were part of the household, the family, or traveled from far away. Many advisors came from the Church itself, as it was the Church that offered education beyond the crafts. Literacy, diplomacy, medicine, and philosophy were taught in religious temples as there were no secular schools at the time.

However, these advisors that the king gathered around him were more than that. They were also witnesses to various charters the king would issue, thus making them legitimate. It is these lists of charter witnesses that proved to be an abundant source of information for historians. From them, we can learn about the social and political network of a royal court. We can learn about the gender and ethnicity of individuals who surrounded the kings. Most of all, the witness lists are an excellent source of information about the king's genealogy, as the members of the royal family are frequently mentioned in them. Furthermore, we know for certain that the choice of witnesses wasn't random. It depended on the subject of the charter, who it concerned, and who was drafting it. For example, a charter that dealt with a daughter's dowry was usually witnessed by the family and kin, while the charters that concerned the Church's land were usually witnessed by the clerics or ealdormen.

The specific roles of the members of the royal households, such as stewards, seneschals, butlers, and sword polishers, were not common during this period, though they did exist in the form of servants during the early medieval period. The Anglo-Saxon courts were itinerant courts, which means the king and the whole household often moved from one residency to another. Because of this nomadic type of government, the royal household couldn't be large. There are two main reasons why the courts had to move around the kingdom like this: to govern the whole kingdom and to check on food stores.

Traveling in this manner allowed kings to have better surveillance of their kingdom. In order to control the magnates, the king had to be present. The government of the Early Middle Ages relied on personal relationships, as it did not have a developed administration for all geographical areas. The king had to deal with his subjects personally, and in order to do so, he had to move. Over time, however, the government changed into a centralized one, which happened when the capital cities started their development and oral tradition changed into a written one.

However, having an itinerant court didn't mean there was no courthouse in which a king could show off all the splendors of royalty. Instead of having a castle to rule from, the kings of the Early Middle Ages had a number of residences, and each one of them was a contemporary wonder. The Mercian courts were richly decorated, as it was expected of a king to dazzle his allies, subjects, and enemies with the display of his power. And how better to display one's power than through rich material culture? Fine clothes, gold and silver, wall hangings in the form of rich textiles, painted walls, jewelry, armor, and weapons were all present in the residences of Mercian kings. These riches also attracted the aristocracy's youth, who sought the opportunity to prove themselves and step into the king's service.

The king's residences during the 8th century were built out of timber, and they were usually very robust square buildings with annexes at each end. Sometimes the royalty occupied old Roman buildings, which they would repair and maintain. The stone hall was introduced in the 9th century, and the old wooden residencies were given an additional stone building. Oftentimes there was a wooden church next to the royal residency, which was also upgraded to a stone building in a later age. Sometimes it is really difficult to discern whether an excavation site used to be a royal hall or an episcopal hall, as the two were of the same shape and size. In cases like that, archeologists usually rely on finding more items that would help point them in the right direction, such as holy relics or additional buildings. The courts were part of a larger complex of buildings, which, through time, eventually grew into towns with their own defenses. The best description for an Early Middle Ages town would be a fortified settlement.

As mentioned earlier, churches also served as schools, but they weren't the only centers for education. Courts usually had very rich libraries and archives where clerics worked. The ecclesiastical order sent bishops to the courts with the purpose of educating young princes and nobles. In the late 780s, Alcuin congratulated Offa for his efforts in promoting education throughout his kingdom, but we don't have any evidence that any kind of learning was available to the commoners. Literacy was high at the Mercian courts, though, and it was possibly a place where *Beowulf*, the Anglo-Saxon epic poem, was written, as their courts were filled with an appropriate audience for literary works. The language of the Church was Latin, and since it was the clergy that filled the ranks of the scribes and other administrative positions, documents were often written in that language. The kings rarely knew how to read Latin, and these documents often needed to be translated. However, many documents and literary works were written in vernacular in order to be available to the wider audience.

A well-educated leadership wasn't enough to keep a kingdom safe from its enemies. In order to defend the kingdom, a ruler needed soldiers, and Mercia relied heavily on their military accomplishments. Ethelbald and Offa were the first Mercian kings who understood that military recruitment must not rely only on the king and his household. They sought soldiers among the common people as well as among nobles. This was why they implemented obligations on all estates. Each estate holder, be it a nobleman or a member of the clergy, was obligated to help the kingdom by building defenses and bridges, providing the material and labor, and to provide people for military service. The Mercian military campaigns might not have been expensive and grand, but they were necessary in order to bring prosperity to the kingdom. As such, these campaigns needed more than one army that was capable of quickly moving across the kingdom. This was why the Mercians developed a network of fortified towns that served to form a kingdom-wide system of defense as well as centers from which an attack could be launched.

Mercia and the Carolingians

Emperor Charlemagne, work of art by Albrecht Dürer

https://en.wikipedia.org/wiki/Charlemagne#/media/
File:D%C3%BCrer_karl_der_grosse.jpg

Christmas Day in the year 800 was a remarkable milestone in the history of medieval Europe, as it was the day Pope Leo III crowned the Frankish king Charlemagne as emperor. The return of the empire to western Europe spoke about the achievements of this king, who reshaped Europe with his Christian objectives. Charlemagne had an intimate relationship with the Church, and he intended to bring the "glory days" of the old Roman Empire back to Europe but this time through the prism of Christianity and Frankish politics.

This event had a large consequence for Anglo-Saxon England as it was part of the Roman Church and culture. Western European kingdoms shared the same perception of Christian kingship, tradition, and trade. Even though England is an island, it could not survive the medieval period without any connections to the continent. Well aware that they were closely tied to other European kingdoms, the Anglo-Saxon kings had to maintain good relations with their continental neighbors.

The Mercian kings were no exception. They needed connections outside of the Anglo-Saxon community, and they needed the recognition of those who were more powerful than themselves. Charlemagne was one such figure, and it seems that Offa constantly sought to be in good standing with him. Receiving support from Charlemagne was a tremendous achievement, as such a powerful ally would bring prestige and security to any Anglo-Saxon kingdom.

The authority of Charlemagne's empire spread from Saxony to the Italian Peninsula, from the Spanish Marshes to Bavaria and the Balkans. His influence was felt in the neighboring Iberian Peninsula and its Emirate of Córdoba, as well as in the east where the Eastern Roman Empire lay. North Africa and the Near East were dominated by the Abbasid Caliphate, but they were under the Frankish influence as well. Charlemagne's diplomatic ties were vast as they encompassed all of these kingdoms. Furthermore, his grasp stretched to the west, all the way to the Irish kingdoms, and northwest to the Anglo-Saxon kingdoms. It is no wonder Offa wanted such a powerful ally, as Charlemagne could tie him to the rest of the world.

The Mercians and Franks had sufficient enough contact to realize that both kingdoms shared a similar perspective, but they were not really dependent on each other. The elite members of society in both the Frankish and Mercian kingdoms saw the world with the same eyes and had the same aspirations and desires. Their cultural views were very similar, and they had the same grasp of the nature of power. They exercised their authority in the same ways as well, as they were both kingdoms that integrated the Holy Roman Church in the very fabric of their states. It is easy to observe Frankish influence in the Mercian court through various excavation sites, but what is interesting is the appearance of Mediterranean influences in the form of sculptures, like the ones found in the church of Breedon-on-the-

Hill. It must have been through Offa's ties to Charlemagne that Mercia acquired the taste for Mediterranean art.

Some historians suggest that Charlemagne and Offa were equals. However, when we think about the scale of Charlemagne's empire and Offa's Mercia, it is impossible to imagine how they could even be compared to each other. Certainly, Charlemagne did not have direct authority over Mercia, but the power of his empire was threatening. It was only natural for Offa to want to tie himself to such a powerful empire through good relations. The fact that Charlemagne refers to Offa as "brother" and "friend" in his letters does not mean they were equals either. This was the language of diplomacy and goodwill.

The relationship between Charlemagne and Offa wasn't a simple one. In their correspondence, they seem to be friendly and supportive of each other, but the fact is that Charlemagne took Offa's enemies under his protection. The court of the Carolingians protected Ecgberht, the claimant to the throne of Wessex, and Eadberht Praen of Kent, who were both rivals of Offa's proteges. There is even the possibility that Charlemagne helped them both with military assistance and monetary funds when they returned to England. It is obvious the Frankish Empire (Francia) posed a significant threat to Mercia, if not directly, then by interfering in Anglo-Saxon socio-political affairs.

Trade

Besides complex diplomatic relations, Mercia and Francia shared trade agreements. There is even evidence of an embargo on Mercian goods at one point when Charlemagne closed the ports to Offa's traders because he was insulted by Offa's suggestion of a marriage between a Frankish prince and a Mercian princess. The embargo was lifted somewhere before 796, as this is the year when Charlemagne sent a letter to Offa complaining about the length and warmth of the cloaks imported from Mercia. They also had correspondence about the black stone Mercia imported, which was probably used as building materials.

However, through relations with Charlemagne and his vast empire, Mercia gained access to long-distance trade. Luxury goods and raw materials were moved and transported all across Europe and beyond. Scandinavia, the lands of the Slavs, the Eastern Roman Empire, and the Mediterranean region were all within reach of the Mercian traders. In Europe, the trade revolved around some key sites, which were usually built around navigable rivers as it would allow easier transport of goods. Later, such trading posts would develop into towns, which attracted various craft specialists who only added to the trade possibilities. In the Anglo-Saxon kingdoms, such towns usually had a "wic" element in their name, which designated a settlement or a harbor. One such example is Lundenwic, which was an important, strategically placed trading post that grew in today's city of London.

London was and still is a major international market, and it was the heart of the Mercian economy. Because Mercia gained authority over London, the kingdom saw the quickening of commercial progress during the late 7th and early 8th centuries, which brought wealth and prosperity. Because it lies on the banks of the River Thames, London brought a direct connection to Normandy, the Seine River Valley, and the Rhineland (the land along the Rhine River in western Germany). London was also an active slave market, but it was the salt exports that brought the most prosperity to the Mercian economy. Other important exports were closely tied to various craft industries such as textiles, leatherworking, jewelry crafting, and artwork.

The widespread usage of silver coins speaks about the prosperity of the Mercian community. Offa issued his own coins at the same time as Charlemagne did, which indicates that there was a need for an exchange office in order to preserve the economy of Mercia. If Frankish coins were used throughout the kingdom, it might start an economic collapse for Mercia. Instead, Offa saw the opportunity to strengthen the economy by issuing his own coins and allowing the trade with other nations through an exchange on which he would collect interest.

Art and Society in Mercia

In early medieval society, the display of wealth and power was important. It confirmed and enhanced the status of individuals and showed their connections to institutions such as the court and the Church. Connections meant power, and displaying imagery that showed imperial authority was particularly important. Showing off one's connections to Carolingian Europe was also a sign of great prestige.

In the medieval period, Mercian art was almost exclusively tied to religion. It was important to show one's piety, and so, art patrons ordered works that would reflect their religious feelings. The cult of the saints or dead ones flourished in the form of sculptures, which were used in church decorations or to raise commemorative and funeral monuments for departed loved ones. Patrons also thought that gifting works of art to the Church would ensure the salvation of their souls and that the display of their power and riches was an added bonus.

The Church promoted art, as it needed architecture and rich decorations to draw people in and be closer to the image of the divine. Through this closeness, awe was achieved, and with that awe came obedience and piety. This kind of artwork offered the people the opportunity to enter the divine landscape and witness it with their mortal eyes before departing this world. To put it simply, art served religion. However, art evolved and created a life of its own outside of religion.

Artists found various ways of expressing themselves through items used purely in secular lives. Jewelry, richly decorated clothing, armors, and weapons were all just materials for the artists. One could always count on the vanity of the aristocracy, even in the Middle

Ages. The royal family and other nobles had to display their sophisticated tastes, and they took any given opportunity to show off. Zoomorphic decorations were dominant in the décor of the Early Middle Ages, but once the Anglo-Saxon kingdoms opened their borders to continental Europe and regions farther away, the influence of Carolingian and Middle Eastern elements can be seen as well. Vegetation, particularly flower decor, was a certain influence of the Frankish Empire, while the use of more abstract shapes was a sign of exotic influences from afar.

Art always had to serve a purpose during the medieval period. It did not exist simply for enjoyment. Thus, their architecture was another way of expressing the artistic views of the world through both the church and court halls. The royal hall at Northampton, which dates back to the 9th century, is a good example of art expressed through masonry. It is a richly decorated stone hall with beautiful artistic carvings. The furniture of the hall is equally eloquent and beautiful in its representation of various symbols. Its wall tapestries could be compared to today's paintings, as they were displayed on the walls and depicted rich scenes of royal hunts, religious motifs, or stories and myths. However, even tapestries had a purpose; they weren't simply wall decorations. They were displayed on the stone and timber walls of royal residences to keep them warm, acting as a form of insulation and trapping the heat inside.

Even medieval literature served the purpose of either being propaganda or spreading a moral point of view to various layers of society. The main centers for scribes and poets were the monasteries, and one such center was in Mercian Worcester and another one in Lichfield. Books weren't just for storytelling, though, and even if their content was as simple as monastery etiquette, the pages were richly decorated with animal and plant ornaments. Scribes were not simply putting down words; they actually had to go through special training to be able to decorate the pages of the books in religiously appropriate ways. For example, the *Codex Bigotianus*, a Gospel book that originated from Worcester, is richly decorated with various birds and beasts. In particular, the predatory beasts were often used as symbols by Mercian artists, including scribes and metalworkers. Another book, the *Barberini Gospels*, dates from the time of Offa's reign, and it draws heavily on the inspiration from Byzantine manuscript painting. It is decorated with stylized symbols such as the Celtic scroll, animal ornaments, and perpetual lacy adornments, and all of it is done in amazingly rich colors.

Art had the power of conveying the message of one's strength and prestige, and the Mercians understood this power very well. However, it wasn't enough to just display art as a symbol of one's social status. Gift-giving played an important role in spreading art, as well as in making political and religious connections. Warriors who showed their loyalty and courage were often gifted decorated swords and battle axes as signs of gratitude, not to mention as a symbol of the connection between the ruler and his knight. The purpose of the gift was to secure this bond and prolong it until the next battle. When it came to the ladies of the medieval period, they were not exempt from gift-giving. It wasn't just jewelry and clothing that were gifted to ladies and queens as symbols of respect and awe. Personalized prayer books and images of saints were more intimate gifts for a lady, and it reflected the appreciation of women's minds and souls. The fact that some of these women's prayer books were written in Latin, Greek, or Hebrew speaks even more of the availability of education in the Mercian kingdom.

The Women of Mercia

Whenever there is a discussion about the medieval period and the position of women in that society, people often come to the conclusion that it wasn't all that great. And compared to the views we have today, it certainly wasn't. However, in some places, it was better than others.

The Germanic tribes that founded the Anglo-Saxon kingdoms throughout England brought their own traditions and customs.

However, they were also open to change, as they integrated the English people well within their societies. In Mercia, in particular, women had more political freedom than in any other Anglo-Saxon kingdom. There is a series of women who left their own trail in the history of Mercia, from the reign of King Offa until the end of the ealdorman of Mercia.

The first woman of Mercia that we can study in detail must be Cynethryth, Offa's wife and widow. She was a political figure in Mercia, and she did not just witness the charters—she also had coins issued in her own name. In the Middle Ages, coins were a rare honor for the men who ruled as kings, let alone a woman whose husband was a king. It is possible that it was Cynethryth who started the tradition of Mercian queens witnessing the charters as she is the first known to do so. For a woman to be listed as a witness wasn't just uncommon in other Anglo-Saxon kingdoms; it was uncommon throughout medieval Europe too.

The importance of women in the Anglo-Saxon kingdoms was reflected in marriages and family ties. The royal daughters of Mercia were often married off to other kingdoms to form strong alliances and friendships. With their Mercian upbringing, they did not miss the chance to become powerful figures, and if they could not be queens, then they would become abbesses or nuns who influenced the religious life of the citizens. One such amazing woman was the daughter of Coenwulf, Abbess Cwenthryth, who became her father's heir. She inherited the lands and authority that came along with them, and because she was a woman, she was challenged by Archbishop of Canterbury Wulfred. Cwenthryth was compelled to resign, but not before her notorious fight for the right of inheritance became a thing of legend.

However, the most powerful female figure of Mercia must be Ethelfled (Æthelflæd), Lady of the Mercians, after whose death the kingdom finally collapsed. She stood alone as a legitimate female ruler during early medieval Europe, which was mainly ruled by men.

She wasn't a regent to an underaged son or a brother. She gained the respect and trust of her people through her deeds, and she ruled in her own right. Even though Ethelfled is considered to be the last queen of Mercia, she was not the last lady who left an imprint on the history of this territory.

During the earldom of Mercia, a prominent female figure rose in the image of Godiva, Countess of Mercia. She is better known as Lady Godiva and is best remembered in the legend about her defiance toward her husband. In protest of the taxes that her husband, Earl Leofric, the earl of Mercia, implemented, she rode a horse down the streets of Coventry, covered only by her long hair. This legend originates in the 13th century and is highly doubtful. However, her importance and political influence are evident, as she appears as a witness to various charters, and her name is mentioned in the Domesday Book, a great census of all English possessions, which was ordered by William the Conqueror. Lady Godiva is mentioned as one of the few remaining Anglo-Saxon landholders and the only woman in this role.

It is safe to presume that it was a Mercian tradition to bring forth powerful women during medieval times. These were women who carved their names in history, often outside of their assigned duties. They were queens, abbesses, and ladies but also daughters, mothers, and sisters who gave council to their lords. The traditional role of a woman in Mercian society certainly differs from the rest of the Anglo-Saxon kingdoms, and it was these Mercian women who shaped the role of a queen as an acceptable and indeed necessary position in the political life of Europe.

Chapter 5 – The Vikings Are Coming

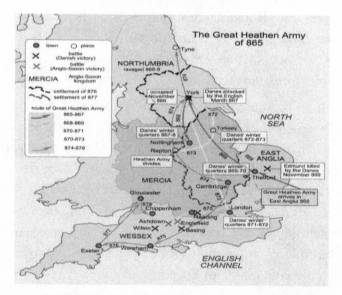

Map depicting the Viking invasion of 865

https://upload.wikimedia.org/wikipedia/commons/thumb/3/35/England_Great_Ar my_map.svg/800px-England_Great_Army_map.svg.png

The Vikings began raiding the British Isles in the late 8th century. The first recorded raid happened in 793 when a monastery at Lindisfarne was attacked and robbed. The *Anglo-Saxon Chronicle* describes the

Vikings as aggressive heathens who came to rob and pillage the British Isles, but it doesn't give us any insight on what was the Viking motivation to do so. There are various theories as to why these attacks happened, but there is not enough evidence to support any of the proposed ideas. Some researchers suggest that the Vikings raided because they needed women. The practice of polygynous relationships led to a shortage of Viking women suitable for the average man. In order to get a woman, an average Viking male had to perform risky tasks due to all the competition and rivalries. Vikings were also used to buying or capturing women, which they would turn into their concubines and wives. The *Annals of Ulster* (medieval Ireland annals) describe how the Vikings plundered an Irish village and then took a great number of women with them.

Other theories suggest the Vikings were plundering in retaliation to the European expansion into their own lands. Charlemagne led a campaign to Christianize Scandinavia, and his policy was to kill anyone who refused baptism. This might have instigated the Vikings to retaliate, but it was the Frankish Kingdom they were angry with, not England. Another idea suggests that there was a great famine that drove the Vikings to search for new areas with fertile land, and even though this might be true for western Norway, as their shores lack fertile ground, there is no suggestion of famine hitting the other parts of Scandinavia. There are many other theories that tried to give an explanation as to why the Vikings raided Britain, but none of them has solid proof. This mystery still remains to be revealed.

In 794, a Viking fleet attacked a monastery at Jarrow, and for the first time in recorded history, they encountered resistance. The Viking leader was killed, and the raiders had to retreat, but they were all killed during their efforts. For the next forty years, the Vikings didn't dare to attack English shores. Even if a small raid did happen, it was easily repelled. That was until 865 when the Great Heathen Army (*mycel hæþen here* in Old English) invaded the Anglo-Saxon kingdoms. This army was a coalition of Scandinavian warriors, mainly Danes, and warbands from Norway and Sweden. Under a unified command, they came to invade and settle, not to raid and pillage like the previous attackers.

The *Anglo-Saxon Chronicle* mentions the four sons of Ragnar Lodbrok (also spelled as Lothbrok) as the commanders of this army: Hvitserk, Ivar the Boneless, Björn Ironside, and Ubba, but they are probably only part of the legend. Nevertheless, the invasion of the Anglo-Saxon kingdoms lasted for the next fourteen years, and it started in East Anglia. Edmund the Martyr, the king of East Anglia, provided the Great Heathen Army with horses in return for peace.

Their first goal was York, which was conquered in 866. After York, the Vikings moved deep into the territories of Mercia.

However, this wasn't the first encounter the Mercians had with the Vikings. During the reign of Beorhtwulf, in 841, the Mercian province of Lindsey was one of the first to suffer from Viking attacks. The next year, London was attacked. The *Anglo-Saxon Chronicle* says that London, a town of great importance for Mercian trade, was badly defeated and that there was a hoard of coins buried somewhere in the vicinity of the town to keep treasures hidden. It was sometime during the first Viking attacks on Mercian territory that Wessex took over the control of Berkshire. It is possible that there was no conflict between Mercia and Wessex, and that an agreement had been made in which Berkshire was given to Wessex. This fact is of great importance, as Alfred the Great, the future king of Wessex, was born in Berkshire at around this time (between 847 and 849).

The second encounter the Mercians had with the Vikings was when a great army of 350 ships landed near Canterbury and London in 851. The attack was so fierce that Beorhtwulf of Mercia and his army had to flee. There is no record of Beorhtwulf's death, but it is presumed that he died somewhere at this point in history as the *Anglo-Saxon Chronicle* now mentions only his successor, Burgred. The Vikings were defeated and driven out of the Mercian lands by

Ethelwulf of Wessex and his sons Ethelstan (Æthelstan) and Ethelbald (Æthelbald).

Burgred became the new king of Mercia in 852, and in the next year, he married the daughter of King Ethelwulf of Wessex, Ethelswith (Æthelswith). With the help of his father-in-law, Burgred managed to subdue the Welsh and quell the rebellion. It was during his reign that the Great Heathen Army arrived in Mercia, after their successful campaigns in Northumbria and East Anglia. In 865, the Vikings started their attack on Mercia, and by 867, they arrived in Nottingham. Burgred couldn't defeat the Vikings alone, and he called for his brothers-in-law, Ethelred of Wessex and Alfred, later known as Alfred the Great, to assist him. The two brothers came to help Mercia but for a price. After they were paid, they did almost nothing to drive the Vikings out, and in 874, Burgred was expelled from his kingdom as the Vikings marched from Lindsey to Repton. Burgred decided to retreat to Rome, where he would later die, but it was not recorded in which year. During this campaign in the Mercian territories, the Viking leader Ivar the Boneless died, and the leadership passed to Guthrum, who conquered Mercia.

It was the Vikings who appointed the next Mercian king, Ceolwulf II, who agreed to pay them with oaths of loyalty. He was the last king of an independent Mercia, and he ruled for five years. Ceolwulf might have been a descendant of Ceolwulf I, but the only tie to the old king was the fact that he carried the same name. However, this might be enough, as it was a custom for the royal family to name their sons with the same prefix "Ceo" (or "Beo" in a different dynasty, which is why historians refer to them as B and C dynasties). Ceolwulf II agreed to surrender his kingdom to the Vikings whenever they called for it, and this happened in 877 when Guthrum, the Viking leader who campaigned in Wessex in 875 and 876, came back to Mercia and claimed some of it. The *Anglo-Saxon Chronicle* describes that Guthrum stayed in the area of Gloucester while leaving parts of the Mercian kingdom to Ceolwulf. In 878,

Guthrum returned to Wessex, but he left a fraction of his army behind to settle in the Mercian lands they had claimed. This is where historians notice that the character of the Vikings attacks changed from violent raiding and pillaging to actually settling the lands, which they started cultivating for their own purposes. Alfred made a deal with Guthrum, in which he allowed the Vikings to keep East Anglia, but he also acknowledged the division of Mercia. The Danes were occupying the eastern provinces while the western part of Mercia was still considered to be under English rule. It was the territory of the old kingdom of Hwicce that was now the heart of English Mercia.

Even though Ceolwulf started his rule as the Viking's puppet king, it seems he tried to regain his independence and form an alliance with Alfred the Great, who became the king of Wessex in 871. In 2015, near Leominster, a large Viking hoard was found. It consisted mostly of Anglo-Saxon jewelry, but unusual coins were found too. Specifically, a coin was discovered that depicted both Ceolwulf and Alfred as equal kings. This suggests a possible alliance between Wessex and Mercia, probably in an effort to expel the Vikings. However, Ceolwulf was quickly forgotten by history, which might indicate that Alfred removed his ally somehow and came out as the sole victor.

In 886, Alfred and Guthrum formalized a treaty, which defined the boundaries between their territories. The Danes now held East Anglia, Northumbria, and parts of Mercia, all territories they had conquered in just a span of ten years. Guthrum agreed to convert to Christianity, and Alfred acted as his godfather. He took a Christian name, Ethelstan, and respected the boundaries set by the treaty with Alfred, and Guthrum turned to rule the eastern territories that were under the Danelaw. The Danelaw is a term used to describe the lands that belonged to the Danes and which responded to the Danish law in contrast to Wessex and English law. The boundary between Wessex and the Danelaw is described in Alfred's treaty as running from the rivers Thames and Lea, up the Ouse to Watling Street.

However, when it comes to the territory of Mercia, it is hard to imagine these boundaries applying to its territory. Historians tend to believe that Mercia presented a problem, as its frontier lay beyond the reach of Alfred's treaty. It seems that the boundary did not follow Watling Street westward; instead, it turned northward at Warwickshire and followed the line that separates Staffordshire, Cheshire, and Lancashire from Derbyshire and Yorkshire. Mercia's northern and eastern parts were now under the Danelaw, and by the early 10th century, these territories were known as the confederacy of the Five Boroughs.

Map of England in 878

https://en.wikipedia.org/wiki/Danelaw#/media/File:England_878.svg

Mercia, as a kingdom, was no more. Its crash under the rule of weak kings and Viking attacks was inevitable. However, Mercia did not cease to exist. Though divided and never to be united under the same name again, Mercia continued to exist as an earldom under the rule of its own lords and ladies, who managed to carve their names in the pages of history with their own greatness.

Chapter 6 – The Rise of Wessex

During 871, in the midst of the Viking attacks, King Ethelred of Wessex died, and his brother Alfred succeeded the throne. Along with the throne, Alfred inherited the burden of defending it from the invaders. Probably taking advantage of the king's death, the Vikings attacked and defeated the army of Wessex at Wilton that same year. Alfred had little hope he would be able to expel the Vikings from his newly acquired kingdom. Instead, the new king decided to negotiate.

Even though there are no remnants of the treaty, Alfred managed to persuade the Danes to leave his kingdom, probably by paying for the peace in coin. The Danes, however, weren't gone for long. They returned in 876 with a new leader, Guthrum, who led his army to Wareham in Dorset. Alfred tried to block them but was unable to win the battle by force. Another peace was then negotiated, and it involved the exchange of hostages, but the Vikings broke their promise, and instead of returning the prisoners, they executed them all. Alfred grew angry and forced the Vikings to submit.

Defeated, they retreated to Mercia for the winter. In January of 878, the Danes attacked Wessex once more, capturing Alfred at Chippenham, where he was spending Christmas. Even though they executed everyone, King Alfred was spared, and later, he managed to escape to the marshes of Somerset. There, he made a fortress at

Athelney, from which he coordinated a counterattack against the Danes in order to regain his kingdom. With the help of the local militia of Somerset, Wiltshire, and Hampshire, Alfred managed to rally enough troops to engage in battle with the Vikings. This is known as the Battle of Edington.

In May 878, Alfred fought the Vikings and was victorious. From his biography written by the monk Asser, we can conclude that Alfred slaughtered the invaders even after the victory was declared, as he pursued them while they were retreating to their fortress. Afterward, he removed all the food the Danes needed inside the fortress in order to survive the siege. After two weeks, it was the Vikings who sued for peace.

Alfred promised he would let them leave his kingdom if their leader Guthrum promised to be baptized. He probably hoped that the doctrine of Christianity would make Guthrum respect the peace treaty and make him an honest Christian king over the lands in the east. Even though this treaty, known to historians as the Treaty of Wedmore, was to be effective immediately, it wasn't signed until much later, after the Mercian king Ceolwulf II was deposed and the division of the Mercian territories happened. This was probably in 879 or 880, and the treaty between Alfred and Guthrum survived in the Old English form and in its Latin translation in the *Quadripartitus* compilation from the 12th century.

Alfred succeeded Ceolwulf on the throne of Mercia, although its northern and eastern parts were now part of the Danelaw. Alfred also gained the incredibly important trade city of London, which had been destroyed by the raids, and part of Essex, with the other part belonging to the Danish. During the reign of Alfred's grandfather, King Ecgberht, Sussex, Kent, and Essex admitted the rule of Wessex, and it seemed they continued to do so.

Even though Guthrum was neutralized as a threat to Alfred's kingdom, he still had to fight other Viking leaders since they all wanted to grab a piece of the land and glory for themselves.

However, these leaders never united against Alfred, and he only had to deal with small skirmishes and raids that never presented a great threat to his kingdom. The largest of these raids was in 885 when the allied kingdom of Kent was under heavy attack. Asser tells the story of Alfred assembling a great army to deal with the Danes at Rochester, but upon seeing the might of Wessex, the Danes fled to the beaches and their ships, choosing to sail away to other parts of Britain instead of facing the wrath of Wessex.

The following year, Alfred was set to restore the city of London to its former glory and make it habitable again. The care of the city was given to his son-in-law, Ethelred of Mercia, the ealdorman who married the king's daughter, lady Ethelfled. Historians agree that it was in this period that all the other Saxon kingdoms and their people submitted to Alfred's rule. He became the "King of England," but he never claimed this title for himself. Even the title "the Great" was given to him much later in the 16th century, making him one of the only two rulers of England to bear that title, with the other king being Cnut the Great. Instead, Alfred used the title *Anglorum Saxonum rex* ("King of the Anglo-Saxons"), recognizing himself as the king of all the English people who were not under the Danish rule.

Alfred's reign from the time of restoring the city of London to the new Viking attacks in the 890s was uneventful, but in 888, his old enemy and the king of East Anglia, Guthrum, died. This event changed the political scene of England, as his death created a power vacuum that stirred up unrest among the power-hungry Viking warlords. Alfred must have known that his years of peace were over. The Danes attacked in the autumn of 892 or 893 when they came from their European settlements with 330 ships. The fact that the Vikings brought their wives and children indicated their intention to conquer and settle. This wasn't just another raid; they meant to stay in the lands they would gain. The Vikings separated themselves into two armies, with one landing at Appledore in Kent, while the other entrenched itself at Milton, also located in Kent. Alfred tried to negotiate with the army at Milton, but the larger body that had been camping at Appledore suddenly attacked. Alfred's son, Edward the Elder, led the army of Wessex, and they were successful in defeating the Danes, who were forced to take refuge on an island called Thorney in the River Colne. This army would later promise to leave Wessex.

At the same time, the Vikings of East Anglia and Northumbria attacked Exeter and the shore of North Devon. Alfred was forced to turn his army and raise the siege of Exeter, leaving his son alone to deal with the Danes who occupied Thorney. Edward wasn't able to contain them alone, but soon, three ealdormen came to help, bringing the forces of Mercia, Wiltshire, and Somerset with them. The Danes failed in their attempt to break the English line of defense and help their fellow Vikings at Exeter. The Vikings who escaped both fronts retreated to Shoebury, where they collected reinforcements and continued to the Roman walls of Chester. Alfred couldn't risk a winter battle and instead satisfied himself with destroying all the supplies his enemies might've been able to use. The lack of food pushed the Danes back to Essex, but at the end of 895, they fortified themselves in the vicinity of London. Even there, they were unsuccessful, as they never managed to cross the river. Alfred outmaneuvered them by blocking the Thames, thus not allowing Danish ships passage through. The next year, the Danes gave up and retired to their own territories in East Anglia and Northumbria. Those who came from Europe in the hopes of settling in the new lands had to return home.

Alfred the Great died in late October of 899, but with his death, Wessex did not diminish. In fact, his son, Edward the Elder, succeeded the throne, and he continued his father's dream of uniting England. As a king, Alfred adopted the title "King of the Anglo-Saxons," as he ruled all the Anglo-Saxon kingdoms that were not under Danish rule. This title passed to his son after he inherited the throne. But Edward achieved so much more than his title suggests.

Instead of limiting himself to ruling Wessex and western Mercia, as they were the only kingdoms that were under Anglo-Saxon law, Edward chose to conquer the territories that were under the Vikings and unite England.

Although there is some evidence that indicates the existence of a conflict between the Anglo-Saxons and the Vikings in the period from 899 until 906, Edward placed emphasis on peace, and he encouraged the English people to settle in Danish territories. He might have planned on resettling Northumbria and East Anglia with the Anglo-Saxons peacefully, but the conflict escalated in 909 when Edward attacked Northumbria in order to relocate the bones of Saint Oswald to Mercia.

Although the Danes had to accept peace at first, they seized the opportunity the very next year to retaliate for this attack. They decided to raid Mercia, but on their way back to Northumbria, they were intercepted by the combined army of Wessex and Mercia, and they suffered a great defeat at the Battle of Tettenhall. The blow to the Vikings was of such magnitude that they never again dared to attack the southern kingdoms. This gave Edward the chance to start conquering East Anglia and eastern Mercia, as well as its Five Boroughs—Derby, Leicester, Lincoln, Nottingham, and Stamford.

Chapter 7 – The Last Queen of Mercia

After the death of Ceolwulf II in 879, Alfred became the ruler of Mercia, but the local administration was passed to Ethelred. The alliance between Wessex and Mercia was sealed by the marriage of Ethelred, Lord of the Mercians, and King Alfred's daughter, Ethelfled. Ethelred's descent is unknown as he does not appear in any of the charters of the previous Mercian kings. He must have had some prestige and influence if Alfred chose to pass the rule of western Mercia to him, though, and his name does suggest a connection to the earlier Mercian kings. It is possible he was the son of King Burgred of Mercia and Alfred's sister Ethelswith; however, if this was the case, then his marriage to Alfred's daughter would have been impossible by Christian laws as they were first cousins. The alternative suggestion is that Ethelred might have been an ealdorman of southwestern Mercia, where the old kingdom of Hwicce used to lie. As such, he could have been influential enough to be granted the title "Lord of the Mercians" after Alfred took the effective rule of the lands. There is some evidence that Ethelred tried to prove his dominance over western Mercia in 881, but by 883, he had accepted Alfred's rule as he realized Wessex was too powerful to allow him to keep the independence of Mercia. This act of Mercia accepting the authority of Wessex was just the first step toward the unification of England. It is the event from which the dream was born, the dream that would continue even after Alfred's death.

There is a disagreement among historians whether Ethelred and Ethelfled bore the title of king and queen or if they were simply regarded as ealdormen of Mercia. This is because some charters that regard the territories of Mercia were issued with the approval of King Alfred, but others were issued independently, without even the mention of Alfred's name. Both Ethelred and Ethelfled issued charters, which suggests that they ruled as equals, as lord and lady. Some suggest Ethelfled was allowed some executive power as she was the daughter of Alfred the Great, but she proved to be more than capable of ruling.

Ethelfled was the first child of King Alfred and his wife, Ealhswith. She was born during the peak of the Viking invasions of Britain. Growing up under constant threat from the Danes, Ethelfled must have learned a lot by observing her father's struggles to keep the last Anglo-Saxon kingdom afloat. Later in life, she would play a major role in the Viking attacks of the 890s because that's when she joined forces with her husband Ethelred and her brother, the future King Edward the Elder. Ethelfled is left out of the *Anglo-Saxon Chronicle*, though, probably because King Edward wanted to diminish her accomplishments in order to discourage the separation of Mercia. She did become a symbol of Mercia's power, and as such, her actions were preserved in Mercian versions of the *Chronicle*. In fact, in this version, her brother is not even mentioned, and her husband is mentioned only as the father of her child, as well as when he died.

All that Mercia achieved between 902 and 924 was attributed to her. Her deeds are also recorded in the Irish chronicle *Three Fragments* but only in the form of legend, not history. Nevertheless, it speaks about her popularity during this period of time. If she was not the queen of Mercia by title, she certainly was by her actions and adoration of the people, whom she fully embraced. Ethelfled was praised by medieval historians William of Malmesbury and John of Worchester, and they gave her more attention than any other medieval secular woman, which attests to her importance.

During her husband's life, Ethelfled never issued a charter in her own name, although she did issue one together with Ethelred with the approval of Alfred the Great. She does appear as a witness to the charters of Ethelred in 888, 889, and 896, and these charters do not have Alfred's name on them. They all concern land and material gifts to the various monasteries in Mercia. The first deed where she is mentioned concerns the reinforcement of Worcester, on which she worked alongside her husband and her brother Edward. When Mercia accepted Alfred's rule, his defensive system of burhs (fortified towns) was extended to Mercia. Worcester was already surrounded by the standing Roman walls, which only needed reinforcements to make them an effective defense. At that time, Worcester was purely the property of the Church, but with the efforts of both Ethelred and Ethelfled, it was transformed into a town that became popular for its craftsmanship. In exchange for their services in reinforcing the walls, the Church gave half of the land to the lordship of Ethelred to be his as long as he was alive but also as long as his wife Ethelfled and their daughter Elfwynn (Ælfwynn) lived. This land was very valuable, as it contained most of the usable river frontage, which enabled the Mercian lords to set up a trade outpost in the town.

Ethelred's health declined rapidly after the death of Alfred in 899, and Ethelfled became the de facto ruler of Mercia. She agreed to the plights of the Norwegian Vikings to settle near Chester after they failed in their Welsh campaign, and for some time, they lived in peace. However, they were in conflict with the Danes, who had the support of the Irish, so Chester was soon attacked. Luckily, Ethelfled fortified that town, and she even managed to persuade the Irish to switch sides. She saved the city through careful planning and the fortification of its Roman walls from the northwest and southeast corners of the fort all the way to the River Dee. It is believed that the later prosperity of the town is because Ethelfled transformed it into a burh.

Ethelfled continued to fortify other Mercian towns and transform them into burhs. One of the most important ones was Gloucester, which became a new minster of importance as the Mercian Witan (council of tribes) was held near it. Its new building wasn't big, but it was rich in décor, which gave it a feeling of grandeur. When King Edward sent the combined Wessex and Mercian armies to raid the Northumbrian Danes, they brought the bones of Saint Oswald to Gloucester, where Lady Ethelfled renamed the minster from St. Peter to St. Oswald in his honor. The love she had for the Gloucester minster is possibly best observed in the fact that she chose it as a resting place for both her and her husband. Gloucester was probably the seat of Mercian power by this time, and the foundation of its church was probably an effort to reinforce the family's importance.

However, The St. Oswald minster wasn't just a church; it was also a place of learning. Education proved to be very important to Alfred, and it is possible that he passed this thought to his daughter, who worked hard on founding minsters. She is also credited with the re-founding of the Chester minster, where she transferred the remains of the Mercian princess Werburgh, who became a saint after her death. In medieval England, it was very important for a church to contain the relics of saints, as it gave prestige to the church. And with this prestige came pilgrimages, education, and trade. However, as the founders, the lord and lady were the ones who profited from this prestige.

Ethelred died in 911, and Ethelfled was elevated to the position of *Myrcna hlaedige*, the "Lady of the Mercians." She officially became the sole ruler of an Anglo-Saxon kingdom, and as a woman in medieval England, it was a special honor and an extraordinary event.

In Wessex, women had no real political power, and even Alfred's wife Ealhswith never held the title of a queen, and she was never mentioned as a witness to the charters. However, in Mercia, the tradition of a queen lived on. Alfred's sister, Ethelswith, was the queen to King Burgred, and as such, she was a witness to the charters. She also made various grants in her own name, not just together with her husband. The tradition of the titular queen in Mercia gave Ethelfled the opportunity to be the ruler and to play an important role in the history of the 10th century. On the other hand, her brother Edward, as the Anglo-Saxon king with the main seat in Wessex, could not allow a queen to overshadow his achievements, and he did all that was in his power to diminish his sister's importance.

Edward took control of some of the profitable towns of Mercia after Ethelred died, such as London and Oxford, which had been granted to Ethelred and Ethelfled by King Alfred. Some of the historians suggest that Ethelfled accepted the losses of these towns in exchange for her brother's recognition of her political position in Mercia. Edward probably granted her this recognition, at least for the time being, as he needed her and the Mercian army in the events that followed. Together, Ethelfled and Edward built a network of burhs across Mercia and Wessex in order to create power bases from which they could control the launches of attacks against the Vikings. Edward must have relied on Ethelfled's ability to guide Mercia and provide him the stability he needed in order to move against the southern Danes. She probably planned and led the campaigns on her own in order to help her brother, as there is evidence of the Mercian army repelling various Viking attacks.

At this point in history, Ethelfled was solely responsible for fortifying Bremesburh (today's location unknown), and by 912, she built defenses around the crossing of the River Severn at Bridgnorth. She built forts at Tamworth in 913, which served the purpose of establishing a defense against the Danes from Stafford and Leicester.

The next year, Ethelfled ordered the fortification of Warwick to help with the defense against the Danes of Leicester, who continued their attacks. Probably in the same year, or shortly before, the defenses of Hereford and Shrewsbury were built. There are many more locations that Ethelfled fortified, but they are all mentioned by their old names in the *Anglo-Saxon Chronicle*, and so, their modern locations remain unknown.

In 917, the Vikings attempted the invasion of Mercian lands by sending three separate armies, but they all failed, as Ethelfled sent an army to capture Derby and all the strategically important territories around it. Derby was one of the Five Boroughs of the Danelaw, and it was the first to fall under English rule. During the battle for Derby, Ethelfled lost four of her *thegns* (lords who served the king during wars) and advisors. This victory, the first of its kind, shows that Ethelfled was a competent leader. The victory at Derby was possibly her greatest triumph, and it was due to her achievement that, at the end of the year, the East Anglian Danes submitted to Edward. In 918, Ethelfled gained Leicester, and the Danish army that was settled there submitted to her. The Vikings of York were ready to pledge their loyalty to her as well, but she died before this could happen. Her brother King Edward never received a similar offer, which testifies to Ethelfled's greatness.

There are not many sources that shed light on Ethelfled's relations with the Welsh. There is a record of the events from 916 when she sent the Mercian army to the Welsh territories in order to avenge the murder of a Mercian abbot. The report tells us her army destroyed the royal residency at Llangorse Lake in the Kingdom of Brycheiniog in southern Wales. The *Anglo-Saxon Chronicle* informs us that after Ethelfled's death, Edward received offers from Welsh kings regarding their submission. This might indicate that prior to her death, the Welsh were indeed under Mercian control.

Neither Ethelfled nor her husband Ethelred issued their own coins in Mercia. However, after 910, a strange silver penny emerged with an unusual ornamental design. It might be that Ethelfled tried in some way to distinguish her own coinage from King Edward's. The evidence that she ruled as a queen of Mercia was supported by the fact that there were no charters issued by Edward between 910 and 924 that are of any concern to Mercia. Ethelfled, on the other hand, did issue charters in her own name, and two of them survived, the first one dating from 914 and the second from 915.

The last queen of Mercia died on June 12th, 918, and she was buried next to her husband in the Gloucester minster of St. Oswald. She died only two months prior to the complete conquest of the southern Danelaw by her brother King Edward. Upon her death, the title of "Lady of the Mercians" went to her daughter, Elfwynn, but soon after, she was deposed from the position as her uncle took Mercia under his direct control. The Mercians did not like their kingdom being incorporated into the rule of Wessex, and they rebelled in resentment. However, Edward managed to put down the rebellion before his death in 924.

Chapter 8 – Mercia the Earldom

After her mother's death, Elfwynn became the titular Lady of the Mercians, but only for a few months, as her uncle King Edward the Elder took her to Wessex and proclaimed his sole rule over Mercia in December 918. There is no written evidence that there was any resistance to Edward, at least not at first. This might mean that Elfwynn didn't have the support of the Mercian nobles like her mother did. There are accounts of a Mercian rebellion from a later date, probably because the kingdom fought to keep its semi-independent status. It must have succeeded in some way, as there are records of Mercia being a separate kingdom under the rule of Ethelstan, the son of King Edward.

When Edward died in 924, the throne of Wessex went to Elfweard (Ælfweard), Edward's younger son and Ethelstan's half-brother. Unfortunately, he died only three weeks after his father. Ethelstan, who already ruled Mercia, became the king of the Anglo-Saxons, and he ruled as such until 927. Mercia was finally fully incorporated into the Kingdom of England, and it became one of its earldoms. It was King Ethelstan who, in 927, conquered York, and in 928, he annexed Northumbria as well as Wales and Cornwall. By doing so, he fulfilled his grandfather's dream of a united England. He ruled as the king of the English from 927 until his death in 939.

Mercia remained an entity that could be identified separately from their English rulers. They were regarded as part of a much larger kingdom, and no independence came to these territories ever again. However, Mercia, as an entity, continued to spread its influence to the other parts of England, this time through culture and kinship. In the early 10th century, Mercia was introduced to the division of territories into shires, a practice that had already been well established in Wessex. This could mean that Mercia was gradually incorporated into a larger kingdom, instead of undergoing the forceful assimilation that an overlordship would bring.

A shire is a basic area of local jurisdiction that was overseen by a local sheriff, who was a royal official. Furthermore, a shire was divided into smaller local entities named "hundreds." Mercia continued to use its tribal names for geographical landmarks, such as the Magonsaete, which is mentioned in a charter from 958, or the Wreocensaete, mentioned in a grant from 963. The Mercian tradition remained strong, though, as the burhs continued to form the main infrastructure of the earldom. The only new thing that came with their incorporation into the larger Kingdom of England was the extent to which these burhs functioned. Further construction of the fortifications continued, and this attracted more and more people, who settled in these burhs or in their vicinity, thus bringing crafts and trade with them. Many of these burhs acted as religious centers as well, and after the division of the kingdom into shires, they continued to do so with the addition of broader responsibilities.

Worcester saw this transition early in the 10th century when it passed from an ecclesiastical burh to a secular one. In the later years of the 10th century, many other religious centers underwent similar transformations where their roles expanded from being purely ecclesiastical to playing an important role in trade and crafts.

The shires were also formed in the eastern parts of Mercia, which was previously under the Danelaw. The Five Boroughs situated at the key points of the road network became the centers of the shires.

Some boroughs transformed into central towns of the shire before others did. For example, Derby, Nottingham, Stamford, and Lincoln transformed during the late 10th century when Northamptonshire, Bedfordshire, and Huntingdonshire already existed. Some shires failed in their transformation, as their position was probably of no importance, and they were later absorbed by other more significant shires. For example, Winchcombe and Stamford were not successful as shires, and they were incorporated into Lindsey.

The Ealdormen and Earls of Mercia

The identity of the Mercians continued to exist mainly because of the fostered tradition of giving allegiance to one leader. After the incorporation of Mercia into the Kingdom of England, these leaders were now in the roles of ealdormen and were later called earls. Mercia was now dominated by magnate families instead of kings and queens. These families were active on the wider political stage of the whole kingdom, but their prime concern lay in their own regions or earldoms. This is where their power bases were and from where they ruled. They were the part of the aristocratic society of the Kingdom of England, and they played a complex game of tenure, patronage, and kinship, which bound them all together to the service of a king.

In return for their service, the king awarded the most loyal ealdorman with various patronages. Only the men from loyal families whom the king could trust were appointed as the ealdorman. It was King Edmund I of England who revived the office, as there had been no ealdormen in Mercia since the death of Ethelred, though it is not certain that he carried this title at all. The first recorded Mercian ealdorman was Elfhere (Ælfhere), who came from a West Saxon family. Elfhere wasn't alone, as his earldom occupied only the territories of the old kingdom of Hwicce, which formed the central area of Mercia. The northwestern parts of Mercia belonged to Ealdorman Ethelmund (Æthelmund), while the provinces to the southeast were held by Ealdorman Ethelstan (Æthelstan). Elfhere was usually the first witness of the charters of King Edgar the

Peaceful, who was the son of Edmund I, from 959 to 975, which gives the impression of Mercia's importance in the Kingdom of England.

In the work of Abbot Byrhtferth of Ramsey, *The Lives of St Oswald and St Ecgwine*, Elfhere is referred to as the "prince of the Mercian people," which speaks of the individuality the Mercians preserved even after their unification under the Kingdom of England. After the death of Elfhere, Elfric Cild (Ælfric Cild), possibly Elfhere's brother-in-law, took the title of Mercian ealdorman; however, after only two years, he was deposed by King Ethelred II the Unready (r. 978–1013, then again ruled 1014–1016). The title fell into abeyance until the renewed Viking attacks in 1007. Due to the pressure from the Viking raids, King Ethelred needed trustworthy people by his side, and the position of ealdorman of Mercia was given to his favorite, Eadric Streona. By 1013, Ethelred II was forced into exile when King Sweyn Forkbeard of Denmark took control over Northumbria, Mercia, and East Anglia, although Ethelred came back after the death of Sweyn Forkbeard to rule England for two more years.

After Ethelred's death in 1016, the role of Mercia, now under the reign of Edmund Ironside, was one of betrayal and uncertainty. Mercian Ealdorman Eadric Streona surrendered to Cnut the Great of Denmark, Sweyn Forkbeard's son, who eventually became the king of Denmark, as well as England and Norway. Eadric was accused of undermining the efforts of the English army on more than one occasion, and it is no wonder he was greatly mistrusted by the English king. First off, he had joined Cnut in 1015, abandoning England. He later rejoined Edmund Ironside in 1016 only to abandon him once more during the Battle of Ashingdon, also known as the Battle of Assandun, and Eadric then joined Cnut for the second time. The *Anglo-Saxon Chronicle* depicts Eadric Streona with obvious resentment, but historians often wonder if his behavior was just a reflection of Mercia's continuous efforts to gain some form of independence. Edmund Ironside died after only six months of ruling, and the whole Kingdom of England fell under the dominion of Cnut the Great.

In 1017, Eadric Streona was confirmed as the ealdorman of Mercia by his new king. At the same time, England was divided into four large earldoms, but the tile of ealdorman was changed to the Scandinavian form—earl. The four new earldoms acted as administrative units of groups of shires, and geographically, they were divided into the territories of the old Anglo-Saxon kingdoms of Wessex, Northumbria, Mercia, and East Anglia. But this division did not last for long as the Anglo-Saxon earls soon fell out of Cnut's favor, and he executed them, thus dividing the earldoms into smaller administrative units, which he gave to the people he trusted the most. Eadric Streona was executed in 1017 on the accusation of betrayal. Cnut probably realized he couldn't trust a man who changed sides so often and who was chronically treacherous.

So, Mercia passed to one of the leading families of the region, and Leofric became the next earl. He is mostly remembered in history as the husband of Lady Godiva, and Mercia stayed in his family's possession until the Norman invasion. The later years of Mercia saw the rise of the Godwinson family, whose earldom was Wessex. Under their ambitious rule, Mercian integrity was threatened, and its territories quickly eroded. The earldoms were frequently reshaped during the years of the Norman Conquest until their boundaries became unrecognizable.

Mercia continued to exist as a significant part of the Kingdom of England, but after the Normans and the rise of William I, better known as William the Conqueror (r. 1066-1087), as the king of England, any dream of independence must have been crushed. Initially, Mercia stayed in the hands of the Old English family of Leofric, but William had to reward the Norman lords who helped him in the conquest, and so, the title and its lands would not remain in the family for very long.

Mercia ceased to exist with the death of Edwin, its last earl and the grandson of Leofric and Lady Godiva. Edwin proved to be of Mercian stock when he got involved in the rebellion against William's rule, displaying the last remnants of Mercia's stubborn demand for autonomy. However, he was betrayed by his own Mercian people and was killed during his flight to Scotland. After him, Mercia was fully integrated into the Kingdom of England, and it did not exist again as an administrative geographical unit. Instead, it was broken and shared between the power-hungry Norman lords who knew nothing of its separatist character and distinctive spirit.

Conclusion

During the 11th century, in the times of the Norman Conquest, the language of Middle English emerged as the dominant one. This was the Mercian dialect, and it can be seen as their last effort toward independence and dominance over all of England. In the later Middle Ages, the Mercian dialect was predominant in the London area, and it was this Mercian dialect that eventually evolved into the modern English language we speak today. It is almost as if the Mercians of old are still defying the natural order and are still striving for conquest and rule. It is as if they are proudly mocking the whole world from their resting places, yelling, "We are still alive!" Through their culture and language, these people of "boundaries" are still influencing our lives, and modern culture is filled with examples. For example, the late Oxford professor of philology and the author of *The Lord of the Rings*, J. R. R. Tolkien used the language of the Kingdom of Mercia to create the fictional language of the Rohirrim.

Mercia was one of the most powerful kingdoms in Anglo-Saxon England. However, there is something mystical and legendary about the Mercians and their heroes. Perhaps it's the lack of written evidence or the depiction of Mercian rulers as notorious warlords in modern representations, but Mercia continues to intrigue us. It began as a simple kingdom that sprouted from the movement of

Germanic tribes to become the most powerful force on the British Isles. It was only natural to see its end. However, its collapse wasn't sudden and total. Mercia, as an earldom, continued to bring influence to the cultural and political scene of the Middle Ages. Even the Norman Conquest didn't manage to crush Mercia's rebellious spirit. Through stories, myths, and legends, the Mercians survived, and we still look to the old days of Mercian power in search for inspiration and guidance.

References

Ashley, M., & Lock, J. (1998). *The Mammoth Book of British Kings & Queens: The Complete Biographical Encyclopedia of the Kings and Queens of Britain*. New York: Carroll & Graf Publishers.

Åberg Nils. (1975). *The Anglo-Saxons in England during the Early Centuries after the Invasion*. Hildesheim: G. Olms.

Breay, C., & Story, J. (2018). *Anglo-Saxon Kingdoms: Art, Word, War*. Londres: The British Library.

Graham-Campbell, J. (2016). *Vikings and the Danelaw*. Place of publication not identified: Oxbow Books.

Hill, D., & Worthington, M. (2005). *Aethelbald and Offa: Two Eighth-Century Kings of Mercia: Papers from a Conference Held in Manchester in 2000: Manchester Centre for Anglo-Saxon Studies*. Oxford: Archaeopress.

Jones, G. (1984). *A History of the Vikings*. Oxford: Oxford University Press.

Loyn, H. R. (1967). *Alfred the Great*. London: Oxford University Press.

Ashley, M., & Lock, J. (1998). *The Mammoth Book of British Kings & Queens: The Complete Biographical Encyclopedia of the Kings and Queens of Britain*. New York: Carroll & Graf Publishers.

Ashley, M. (1961). *Great Britain to 1688, A Modern History*. Ann Arbor: University of Michigan Press.

Carruthers, B., & Ingram, J. (2013). *The Anglo-Saxon Chronicle*. Barnsley: Pen & Sword.

Finberg, H. P. (1964). *The Early Charters of Wessex*. Leicester: Univ. Press.

Keynes, S., & Lapidge, M. (2004). *Alfred the Great: Asser's Life of King Alfred and Other Contemporary Sources*. London: Penguin Books.

Young, G. M. (1934). *The Origin of the West-Saxon Kingdom*. London: Oxford University Press, H. Milford.

Here's another book by Captivating History that you might be interested in

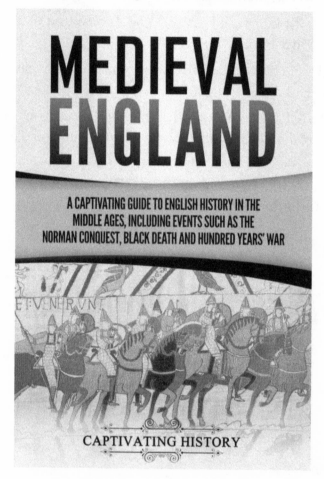